Working with the ADHD Brain

(Parent Edition)

A Parent's Guide to Building Focus, Organization, and Academic Success

Patty R. Adams

Table of Contents

Thank You for Reading!

I hope you found *Working with the ADHD Brain (Parent Edition): A Parent's Guide to Building Focus, Organization, and Academic Success* helpful and enjoyable!

Your feedback is invaluable to me and helps others discover this book.

If you could take a moment to **leave a review**, I'd greatly appreciate it. Scan the QR code below to leave your review:

Thank you,

Patty R. Adams

Introduction

Have you ever watched your child's eyes fill with tears over homework that seems simple to everyone else? Maybe you've spent hours creating organizational systems, only to find assignments still lost and deadlines still missed. Or perhaps you've lain awake at night wondering why traditional parenting advice just doesn't seem to work for your bright, capable child.

As a school counselor with nearly four decades of experience, I've sat with thousands of parents just like you; dedicated caregivers who feel caught in an exhausting cycle of reminders, consequences, and frustration. Parents who've tried every strategy in the book, yet still find themselves wondering: "Why can't my kid just get it together?"

Here's what I want you to know right now: Your child isn't choosing to struggle. Their brain is wired differently, processing information and managing tasks in unique ways that often clash with traditional expectations. But understanding this difference, really understanding it, can transform your approach to supporting their success.

This isn't another book about fixing your child or forcing them to fit a mold that wasn't designed for them. Instead, we're going to explore how the ADHD brain actually works, and more importantly, how to work with it rather than against it. You'll discover practical, science-backed strategies that harness your child's natural strengths while building crucial skills for focus, organization, and emotional regulation.

Through my years of counseling, I've witnessed remarkable transformations when parents shift from fighting against ADHD to embracing their child's unique operating system. Like Sophie, who went from hiding incomplete assignments in her backpack to confidently managing her homework using methods that matched her visual learning style. Or Marcus, whose chronic disorganization transformed into capability once we created systems that actually made sense to his ADHD brain.

In the pages ahead, you'll find real solutions for your daily challenges: managing homework without meltdowns, creating organization systems that stick, building effective study habits, and advocating for your child at school. These aren't just theories; they're proven strategies tested in classrooms and homes, refined through decades of working with students and families just like yours.

Most importantly, you'll discover that your child's different way of thinking isn't a deficit to be corrected; it's a unique perspective that, when properly supported, can lead to incredible achievements. Together, we'll explore how to create an environment where your child can thrive, focus, and succeed while staying true to who they are.

Let's begin this journey of understanding and practical solutions. Because with the right tools and insight, you can help your child not just "get it together," but soar in ways you never imagined possible.

Chapter 1:

The ADHD Brain Blueprint: Understanding Your Child's Unique Operating System

Every child's brain is uniquely wired, but the ADHD brain operates on a distinctly different operating system; one that processes information, manages time, and responds to stimuli in its own special way. Understanding this unique neural architecture isn't just about knowing what makes your child different; it's about discovering how to work with their natural tendencies rather than against them. "Sometimes the smallest shift in perspective can lead to the biggest breakthrough in understanding." These words have guided my approach throughout my four decades as a school counselor, especially when helping parents understand their children with ADHD.

In this chapter, we'll explore the intricate workings of the ADHD brain, not as a problem to be fixed, but as a unique operating system that requires its own special set of instructions to function optimally. We'll delve into the science behind executive functions, the role of neurotransmitters, and how attention regulation works differently in the ADHD mind, all through the lens of practical, everyday experiences.

During my early years as a school counselor, I worked with a bright student named Aurora who struggled with completing tasks and staying organized. Her parents were frustrated, believing she was simply being defiant or lazy. One day, I asked Aurora to describe how her mind worked when trying to complete homework. She painted a vivid picture: 'It's like having 100 TV channels playing at once, and someone else keeps changing the channel every few seconds.' This metaphor became a turning point in how her parents understood her experience. Instead of fighting against Aurora's different operating system, they began working with it; breaking tasks into smaller chunks, creating visual schedules, and incorporating movement breaks. Within months, Aurora's confidence soared, and her academic performance improved significantly.

This experience taught me a fundamental truth: when we truly understand how the ADHD brain works, we can transform struggles into strengths. It's not about forcing a square peg into a round hole; it's about recognizing that different shapes require different openings.

As we move through this chapter, you'll discover why traditional approaches to learning and organization often fall short for children with ADHD. We'll examine the delicate balance of brain chemistry, particularly focusing on dopamine's crucial role in attention and motivation. But more than just understanding the "why," you'll learn how to use this knowledge to create effective strategies that work with your child's natural tendencies.

Think of your child's brain as a sophisticated computer running on a unique operating system; not a broken version of a typical brain, but a different configuration altogether. Just as you wouldn't try to run

Windows software on a Mac without proper adaptation, we need to adjust our approaches to match how your child's brain naturally processes information and responds to the world.

As we explore these concepts, you'll begin to recognize patterns in your child's behavior that suddenly make perfect sense. Those moments of intense focus on preferred activities? There's a neurological explanation for that. The difficulty transitioning between tasks or keeping track of time? We'll uncover the brain-based reasons behind these challenges and, more importantly, how to work with them effectively.

This understanding isn't just theoretical; it's transformative. When we grasp how the ADHD brain processes information differently, we can begin to create environments and systems that support rather than hinder our children's natural way of learning and growing. Through this knowledge, you'll discover that your child's unique brain wiring isn't a deficit to be overcome, but a difference to be understood and leveraged for success.

The Executive Function Command Center: Understanding Your Child's Brain Management System

Picture your child's morning routine: getting dressed, packing a backpack, remembering to grab lunch, and making it to the bus on time. For most children, these tasks flow naturally. But for a child with ADHD, this seemingly simple sequence can feel like coordinating a complex space mission without a control center.

This is where executive function comes in: your child's brain's management system. Think of it as an air traffic controller responsible for coordinating multiple "flights" of thoughts, actions, and emotions.[1] In children with ADHD, this control center operates differently, creating unique challenges in organizing, planning, and completing daily tasks.[2]

The executive function system, primarily located in the prefrontal cortex, manages six essential skills:[3]

- Working Memory: Holding and using information in the moment
- Cognitive Flexibility: Adapting to new situations and switching between tasks
- Inhibitory Control: Resisting impulses and staying focused
- Task Initiation: Getting started on activities
- Time Management: Understanding and planning for time demands
- Emotional Regulation: Managing feelings and responses

When I explain this to parents, I often use the analogy of a symphony orchestra. In a typical brain, the conductor (executive function) coordinates all the instruments (thoughts, actions, emotions) to play in harmony. In the ADHD brain, it's as if the conductor is trying to lead the orchestra while standing on a moving platform; the musical talent is there, but coordinating everything becomes more challenging.

Research shows that children with ADHD typically show decreased activity in their prefrontal cortex during tasks requiring executive control.[4] This isn't a matter of trying harder; it's about their brain's unique operating system processing information differently.

This knowledge transforms how we view daily challenges. That homework assignment that never makes it from backpack to teacher? That's not irresponsibility; it's an organizational challenge rooted in executive function differences. The morning routine that dissolves into chaos? It's not defiance; it's a working memory and sequencing challenge.

Understanding these neurological differences helps us move from frustration to effective action. Instead of saying, "Why can't you just remember?" we can ask, "How can we create systems that support your brain's natural way of working?"

Let's look at a practical example: Sarah, a student I worked with, struggled with completing multi-step projects. Rather than assuming she was unmotivated, we recognized this as an executive function challenge. We created a visual project map, breaking each assignment into clear, manageable steps with built-in checkpoints. This approach worked with her brain's needs rather than against them.

The impact of executive function differences extends beyond academics into every aspect of daily life, from managing emotions to navigating social situations. However, understanding these differences is the first step toward developing effective strategies and support systems that actually work for your child's unique brain wiring.

By the end of this section, you should understand that your child's executive function challenges aren't about laziness or lack of effort;

they're about brain wiring that requires different approaches to succeed. In the following chapters, we'll explore practical strategies to support each executive function skill, but first, let's pause for a moment of reflection:

Consider your child's daily routines. What tasks seem particularly challenging? How might understanding these as executive function differences rather than behavioral choices change your approach?

Remember: Executive function isn't just about getting organized or staying focused; it's about how your child's brain processes and manages information, emotions, and actions. When we understand this fundamental truth, we can begin to create environments and systems that support rather than hinder their natural way of learning and growing.

Dopamine and Motivation: The Brain's Reward Highway

Picture your child's brain as a complex highway system, where dopamine acts as the fuel that powers motivation and focus. For children with ADHD, this highway operates differently than in neurotypical brains, creating unique patterns in how they experience reward and maintain attention.[5]

Think of dopamine as the brain's reward messenger; it signals when something is worth our attention and effort.[6] In the ADHD brain, this messaging system works differently. It's like having a fuel gauge that doesn't accurately show how much gas is left in the tank, making it harder to maintain steady motivation for tasks that don't provide immediate rewards.[7]

This explains why your child might hyperfocus on video games while struggling to start homework. Video games provide instant, consistent dopamine feedback, while homework offers delayed, less predictable rewards. It's not about willpower or defiance; it's their brain's natural response to different types of motivation.[8]

Research shows that children with ADHD often require stronger, more immediate rewards to experience the same motivational effects as their peers.[9] This isn't a character flaw; it's their brain's unique operating system at work.

Understanding this difference transforms how we approach motivation. Instead of relying on distant rewards like good grades or weekly allowance, we can create systems that provide more immediate positive feedback. For instance:

- Breaking large tasks into smaller, quickly achievable goals
- Incorporating movement and novelty into routine activities
- Creating visual progress trackers that offer frequent wins
- Using timer challenges to make tasks more engaging
- Providing immediate positive reinforcement for effort

The key is working with your child's natural reward system rather than against it. When Lucy, a student I counseled, struggled with math homework, we transformed it into a "beat the timer" game with small celebrations for each completed problem. This wasn't about bribing her to do work; it was about aligning the task with how her brain naturally processes motivation.

This knowledge helps us move past judgment and toward effective solutions. Your child isn't being difficult when they struggle to maintain motivation for "boring" tasks; their brain literally processes reward and motivation differently than their peers.[8]

By understanding this dopamine difference, we can create environments that support rather than fight against their natural tendencies. This might mean:

- Making abstract goals more concrete and immediate
- Adding elements of fun or competition to routine tasks
- Celebrating effort and progress, not just final outcomes
- Using technology tools that provide immediate feedback

Remember, the goal isn't to change how your child's brain works; it's to work with their unique reward system to help them succeed. When we understand the role of dopamine in motivation, we can transform daily challenges into opportunities for success.

Most importantly, this understanding cultivates empathy. Those moments of seeming "laziness" or "lack of effort" are often simply expressions of how the ADHD brain processes motivation differently. With this knowledge, we can move from frustration to effective support, creating systems that help our children thrive.

As you reflect on this section, consider: How might understanding your child's unique reward system change your approach to motivation? What small changes could you make to better align tasks with how their brain naturally processes reward?

Attention Regulation: Why Focus Feels Different for ADHD Minds

Think of focus like a spotlight in a dark theater. In most brains, this spotlight moves smoothly between important tasks, naturally dimming distractions in the background. But in the ADHD brain, this spotlight works differently; it might flicker between multiple points of interest, suddenly intensify on unexpected details, or struggle to stay fixed on what's meant to be center stage.

This unique attention pattern isn't a matter of choice or willpower; it's rooted in how the ADHD brain processes and filters information. Research shows that children with ADHD have distinct differences in how their brains regulate attention through key neural networks.[10] The prefrontal cortex, which acts as the brain's attention control center, functions differently in ADHD minds, affecting how they process and prioritize incoming information.[12]

Jake, a student I worked with, once described his experience: "It's like trying to listen to someone whisper while there's a marching band playing nearby; except sometimes the whisper feels as loud as the band, and I can't tell which one I'm supposed to pay attention to." This perfectly captures how the ADHD brain often processes all stimuli with similar intensity, making it challenging to naturally filter out what's less important.

The science behind this experience reveals that the ADHD brain's default mode network (DMN), the brain's 'daydreaming' system, remains unusually active during tasks that require focus.[11] It's as if the brain's "mind wandering" channel keeps playing even when it should be quiet, making it harder to maintain consistent attention on demand.

This different attention regulation system creates both challenges and unique strengths. While it may make it difficult to focus during a quiet reading session or lengthy lecture, it can also enable periods of intense focus (hyperfocus) when engaged in stimulating activities.[13] Understanding this helps explain why your child might struggle to complete homework but can spend hours deeply absorbed in building with LEGOs or creating art.

The emotional impact of these attention differences shouldn't be overlooked. When children repeatedly struggle to maintain focus in situations where others seem to do so effortlessly, it can lead to frustration and self-doubt. That's why it's crucial to understand that their experience of attention isn't a character flaw; it's a result of real neurobiological differences in how their brains process and prioritize information.

Effective support strategies work with, rather than against, this unique attention system:

- Breaking tasks into shorter, more manageable segments
- Creating environments that minimize competing stimuli
- Using tools like timers and visual schedules to externalize time
- Incorporating movement and sensory input strategically
- Recognizing and working with periods of natural focus

When we understand these attention differences, we can transform how we support children with ADHD. Instead of constant reminders to "pay attention," we can create environments and routines that work with their natural attention patterns.

Consider Maria, a fourth-grader who struggled with completing independent reading. Once we understood her attention regulation differences, we adapted her reading routine to include short movement breaks, a fidget tool for her hands, and an audiobook to support her visual reading. These changes didn't fix her attention regulation; they worked with it, allowing her natural abilities to shine through.

Remember: The goal isn't to make your child's attention system work like everyone else's. It's about understanding and supporting their unique way of engaging with the world. When we shift from trying to fix attention differences to working with them, we open the door to more effective strategies and greater success.

Take a moment to reflect: How does understanding these attention differences change how you view your child's focus challenges? What environments or activities naturally support their attention system, and what can we learn from these successful moments? As we conclude this exploration of the ADHD brain's unique architecture, let's pause to reflect on the transformative power of understanding. Through our journey into executive functions, dopamine's role, and attention regulation, we've uncovered fundamental truths about how your child's mind works, not as a broken system, but as a different operating system with its own special capabilities and needs.

Remember Aurora's story from the beginning of this chapter; how the simple metaphor of "100 TV channels playing at once" helped her parents shift from frustration to understanding? This represents the heart of what we've learned: when we truly grasp how the ADHD brain works, we can transform daily challenges into opportunities for success.

Let's recap our key insights:

- The ADHD brain isn't deficient; it's differently wired with unique patterns of processing information and managing tasks
- Executive function differences affect how your child organizes thoughts, manages time, and regulates emotions
- Dopamine's unique role explains why traditional motivation systems often fall short
- Attention regulation isn't about willpower; it's about fundamental differences in how the brain processes and prioritizes information.

But understanding these differences is just the beginning. In the chapters ahead, we'll build upon this foundation to explore practical strategies that work with your child's natural tendencies rather than against them. We'll discover how to create environments, routines, and support systems that align with their brain's unique operating system.

Before we move forward, take a moment to reflect on your own journey of understanding:

- What aspects of your child's behavior make more sense now that you understand their brain's unique wiring?
- How might this new perspective change your approach to supporting their daily challenges?

- What strengths have you noticed that might be connected to their different way of processing the world?

Remember, you're not just learning about your child's brain; you're gaining the tools to become their most effective advocate and supporter. By understanding the science behind their experiences, you can create environments and systems that help them thrive.

In the chapters ahead, we'll transform this knowledge into action, exploring specific strategies for harnessing dopamine, supporting executive function, and working with your child's unique attention patterns. But for now, celebrate how far you've come in understanding your child's unique operating system. This understanding is the first step toward meaningful change.

Your journey to supporting your child's success doesn't end here; it's just beginning. Armed with this deeper understanding of the ADHD brain, you're better equipped to navigate the challenges ahead and celebrate the unique gifts your child brings to the world.

Chapter 2:

Dopamine's Dance: Harnessing Natural Motivation for School Success

The morning sun streams through Ruby's bedroom window as she sits at her desk, surrounded by colorful sticky notes, fidget toys, and a visual timer - tools we've carefully chosen to support her ADHD brain. While many parents believe motivation comes from strict schedules and consequences, the secret to unlocking your child's academic potential lies in understanding and working with their brain's natural reward system. "Understanding motivation isn't about pushing harder; it's about aligning with your child's natural reward system." - Dr. Sarah Thompson

During my early years as a school counselor, I worked with a bright student named Ruby who struggled with completing assignments. Traditional motivation techniques, sticker charts, consequences, and constant reminders only seemed to increase her anxiety and resistance. Everything changed when we started understanding her dopamine needs. Together, we broke down her math homework into 10-minute chunks, each followed by a brief movement break. We created a "success station" at her desk with fidget tools and a timer that made time visible. The real breakthrough came when Ruby discovered she could draw small cartoons to explain math concepts. This visual approach not only helped her retain information but also gave her the dopamine boost her brain craved. Within two months, Ruby's math grades improved from D's to B's, not because she became a different person, but because we finally aligned her learning environment with her brain's needs. This experience fundamentally shaped my approach to helping students with ADHD find their academic groove.

The science behind motivation in the ADHD brain reveals a fascinating truth: it's not about willpower or discipline, but about understanding and working with your child's unique neurological wiring. When we grasp how dopamine, the brain's reward and motivation neurotransmitter, functions differently in ADHD brains, we can transform our approach to learning and achievement.

Think of dopamine like fuel for your child's motivation engine. In neurotypical brains, this fuel flows steadily and predictably. But in ADHD brains, it's more like a sporadic sprinkler system; sometimes gushing, sometimes trickling, rarely consistent. This explains why your child can focus intensely on activities they find engaging while struggling to maintain attention on seemingly simple tasks.

In this chapter, we'll explore practical strategies for creating learning environments that naturally boost dopamine production and maintain motivation. You'll learn how to structure tasks, build reward systems that actually work, and create study routines that align with your child's brain chemistry rather than fight against it. Most importantly, you'll discover how to help your child tap into their natural interests and strengths to fuel academic success.

Remember, the goal isn't to change who your child is; it's to create an environment where their unique brain wiring becomes an advantage rather than a hindrance. When we understand the dance of dopamine in the ADHD brain, we can choreograph learning experiences that set our children up for success.

Understanding the Dopamine-Motivation Connection in ADHD Brains

"Have you ever watched the little bubbles in a soda bottle fizz to the top, only to sink back down again? That's a bit like how dopamine works in your child's ADHD brain," I often tell parents during our counseling sessions. "Sometimes there's a burst of energy and focus, other times, it's hard to get any bubbles rising at all."

Dopamine acts as the brain's natural motivator, playing a crucial role in attention, reward, and goal-directed behavior.[15] In typical brains, this chemical messenger flows steadily and predictably. However, research shows that ADHD brains have an underactive dopamine system, particularly in regions associated with motivation and reward processing.[14, 6]

This biological difference fundamentally changes how your child experiences motivation. It's not about being lazy or difficult; their brain literally requires more immediate, intense rewards to experience the same level of drive that their peers might feel naturally. Think of it as needing a stronger signal to get the same message through.

I witnessed this firsthand working with Maya, a bright seventh-grader who struggled with long-term projects. Traditional advice about "keeping her eye on the prize" fell flat because her brain wasn't wired to respond to distant rewards. Everything changed when we restructured her work into smaller, more immediately rewarding chunks. Each completed section earned her a brief break to sketch (her passion), which naturally boosted her dopamine levels. The result? Her first completed science fair project and a newfound confidence in tackling big tasks.

The impact of this dopamine difference shows up in several key ways:

- Your child may find it extremely challenging to persist with tasks that offer delayed rewards.[14]
- They might hyperfocus on activities that provide instant feedback (like video games).[14]
- Traditional reward systems often fall flat because the delayed gratification doesn't trigger sufficient dopamine release.[6]

Research in neuroscience has revealed that children with ADHD often have fewer dopamine receptors and transporters in key brain regions.[6] This means they need stronger stimulation to achieve the same level of motivation as their peers. It's like turning up the volume to hear a quiet song; they need amplified rewards to register the same motivational impact.

This knowledge is transformative because it shifts our perspective from "why won't they just try harder?" to "how can we create an environment where their brain can succeed?" When we understand that motivation isn't about character but chemistry, we can stop fighting against nature and start working with it.

Consider Emma, another student I worked with, who struggled with reading assignments. Instead of forcing her to sit still for 30 minutes, we broke her reading into 5-minute segments, each followed by a quick movement break. We added colorful sticky notes for her to track interesting parts and created a simple points system for each completed section. These weren't arbitrary changes; they were strategic adjustments based on how her brain processed rewards.

The practical implications of this understanding are profound. Instead of lengthy tasks with distant rewards, we need to create systems of immediate feedback. Rather than expecting sustained focus without support, we can build in regular dopamine boosts through movement, novelty, and immediate recognition of progress.[14, 15]

Remember: your child's brain isn't broken; it's uniquely wired. When we align our strategies with this wiring, we create pathways to success that feel natural and sustainable. In the next section, we'll explore practical ways to create reward-rich learning environments that naturally enhance motivation and focus.

Creating Reward-Rich Learning Environments at Home

"The key to motivation isn't forcing compliance, it's creating an environment where success feels natural and rewarding," I often tell parents during our counseling sessions. Every space can become a catalyst for learning when we understand how to align it with the ADHD brain's unique reward system.

Let's explore Zoe's transformation as an example. When I first met Zoe, her study space was a traditional desk setup that felt more like a prison than a learning sanctuary. Together, we reimagined her environment, incorporating elements that naturally boosted her dopamine levels while supporting focus and motivation.[16]

The essential elements of a reward-rich learning environment include:

- Immediate Visual Feedback: We installed a large whiteboard where Zoe could track daily progress and celebrate small wins.[16]
- Strategic Movement Opportunities: We added a therapy ball chair and designated movement zone for quick energy releases.[18]
- Sensory Tools: A carefully curated collection of fidget tools that helped maintain focus without causing distraction.[17]
- Time Management Visuals: We used special timers that made time tangible and visible.[19]
- Choice Stations: Different work areas for different types of tasks, giving Zoe autonomy in her learning process.[17]

The key is creating what I call "dopamine bridges," environmental elements that help maintain motivation between task initiation and completion. For Zoe, this meant breaking her homework space into distinct zones: a "launch pad" for planning, a "focus zone" for concentrated work, and a "celebration station" for tracking progress.[16, 18]

One particularly effective approach is implementing a token economy system that provides a tangible representation of progress while teaching delayed gratification in manageable steps.[19] Tokens can be earned for completing homework tasks, following routines, or demonstrating positive behaviors, then traded in for preferred activities or privileges.

When setting up your reward system, consider these practical guidelines:

- Keep rewards varied and meaningful to your child's interests.[16]
- Rotate options regularly to maintain novelty and engagement.[17]
- Use both immediate and delayed rewards to build tolerance for waiting.[18]
- Make earning rewards achievable but not automatic
- Focus on effort and progress rather than perfection

The physical setup of the space matters tremendously. For instance, we helped Zoe's parents create what we called a "success circle," arranging her desk, supplies, and visual aids in a way that minimized distractions while maximizing access to supportive tools. Everything she needed was within arm's reach, but organized in a way that prevented overwhelm.

Most importantly, stay flexible and observant. What works brilliantly one month might need adjustment the next. The key is to maintain open communication with your child about what helps them feel successful and motivated. Through my decades of experience, I've learned that the most effective learning environments evolve alongside the child's changing needs and interests.

A critical component often overlooked is the power of specific praise alongside tangible rewards. When acknowledging progress, be precise about what behavior you're reinforcing.[16] Instead of a general "good job," try "I noticed how you broke down that math problem into smaller steps; that kind of planning really helps you succeed."

Consider implementing a Daily Report Card system between home and school. This tool provides structured feedback throughout the day and helps maintain consistency across different environments.[18] It breaks the day into manageable chunks, making progress visible and reward opportunities more frequent.

Remember, this isn't about creating dependency on external rewards but about bridging the gap between effort and satisfaction that often exists in the ADHD brain. As your child experiences more success and builds confidence, many of these external supports can gradually be reduced.

I've seen countless students transform their academic experience through thoughtfully designed learning environments. Like Sarah, a tenth grader who went from avoiding homework to independently managing her studies after we created what she called her "focus fort" - complete with ambient lighting, a progressive task board, and strategic break stations.

The goal is to create an environment that works with your child's natural tendencies rather than against them. When we understand that motivation isn't about willpower but about brain chemistry[19], we can stop fighting against nature and start working with it. Your child's learning space should feel like a launch pad for success, not a battleground for compliance.

Building Momentum: Small Wins and Progressive Challenges

"Success isn't about grand leaps forward - it's about steady steps in the right direction," I often remind parents during our counseling sessions. For children with ADHD, those steps need to be carefully calibrated to create a sustainable path toward achievement.

Consider the story of Marcus, a middle school student who struggled with writing assignments. His previous experience with essay writing had left him convinced he couldn't succeed. Rather than focusing on completing entire essays, we started with a goal of writing just one strong sentence. Each sentence became a small win, celebrated and tracked on a visual progress board. As his confidence grew, we gradually increased the challenge - from sentences to paragraphs, from paragraphs to short essays. Within two months, Marcus wasn't just completing assignments; he was actively participating in writing discussions and sharing his work with pride.

The science behind building momentum is clear: each small win triggers a dopamine release, creating a positive feedback loop that reinforces motivation and makes starting the next task easier.[20, 21] Research shows that children with ADHD have different dopamine systems, particularly in areas associated with motivation and reward[24] [21]. This means they need more frequent, immediate feedback to maintain momentum compared to their peers.

Here are essential strategies for creating momentum through small wins:

- Break tasks into micro-steps that feel achievable[20, 21]
- Define clear, specific success criteria for each step[20]
- Use visual tracking systems to make progress tangible[20, 21]
- Celebrate small victories meaningfully and immediately[20, 21]
- Build on existing strengths before tackling challenges[22, 23]

The key is to start where your child already feels confident and gradually increase the challenge level. This approach, known as progressive challenge, helps maintain engagement while building competence[23]. Think of it like adjusting the difficulty settings in a video game - you want each level to be challenging enough to be interesting but not so hard that it becomes frustrating.

One particularly effective approach is the SMART goal framework, adapted specifically for ADHD brains. Goals should be Specific, Measurable, Achievable, Realistic, and Time-bound, but with shorter time horizons than you might use for neurotypical children[23]. Instead of weekly goals, think daily or even hourly targets that provide frequent opportunities for success.

Progressive challenges should follow what experts call the "70/30 rule" - tasks should feel about 70% manageable and 30% challenging[23]. This ratio keeps children engaged while building confidence through regular success experiences. Start with tasks that align with your child's interests and strengths, then gradually introduce more challenging elements.

Consider Emma's journey with math homework. Instead of tackling an entire worksheet at once, we began with three problems she felt confident solving. Once she experienced success, we added one slightly more challenging problem. The key was maintaining that delicate balance between comfort and challenge; enough success to build confidence, enough challenge to maintain engagement.

Remember that autonomy plays a crucial role in maintaining momentum. When children have input in setting their goals and choosing their rewards, they're more likely to stay engaged and motivated.[23] This isn't about creating dependency on external rewards; it's about building bridges between effort and satisfaction until internal motivation can take over.

The goal isn't perfection; it's progress. Each small win builds not just momentum but also resilience and self-belief.[20, 21, 22] When children see themselves succeeding repeatedly, even in small ways, it fundamentally shifts their self-perception from "I can't" to "I can."

Most importantly, stay flexible and observant. What constitutes a "win" will vary from child to child and may change over time. The key is maintaining open communication about what helps your child feel successful and adjusting your approach accordingly. This isn't just about managing tasks; it's about teaching your child to understand and work with their unique brain-wiring in ways that support long-term success.

As you implement these strategies, remember that setbacks are normal and actually provide valuable learning opportunities. Help your child see challenges not as failures but as feedback; information they can use to adjust their approach and try again. This resilience-building mindset, combined with the momentum of small wins, creates a powerful foundation for sustained academic success. As we conclude our exploration of dopamine's vital role in motivation and learning, let's reflect on the transformative power of understanding your child's unique brain chemistry. Throughout this chapter, we've discovered how aligning our approach with the natural reward systems of the ADHD brain can revolutionize academic success.

Remember Ruby's journey; how shifting from traditional motivation techniques to dopamine-friendly strategies transformed not just her grades, but her entire relationship with learning. Her story illustrates a fundamental truth: when we work with our children's natural brain wiring instead of against it, we create pathways to success that feel authentic and sustainable.

Let's recap the key insights that will transform how you support your child's academic journey:

- The ADHD brain requires more immediate, frequent rewards to maintain motivation
- Creating reward-rich environments isn't about bribing; it's about aligning with natural brain chemistry
- Small wins and progressive challenges build momentum through regular dopamine boosts
- Visual tracking systems and immediate feedback strengthen motivation pathways
- Movement, novelty, and choice are powerful tools for maintaining engagement

As you move forward, remember that this isn't about changing who your child is. It's about creating an environment where their unique neural architecture becomes an advantage rather than a hindrance. Every small victory, every moment of engagement, and every successful study session builds not just academic skills but also confidence and self-understanding.

Start by implementing just one strategy from this chapter; whether it's breaking down tasks into dopamine-friendly chunks, creating a visual reward system, or incorporating movement breaks into study time. Remember how Ruby's transformation began with understanding and small adjustments. Your journey with your child starts with these first steps toward alignment with their natural motivation patterns.

In the next chapter, we'll explore how to translate this understanding of motivation into practical organizational systems that support academic success. You'll learn how to create structures that work with your child's brain, not against it, setting the stage for lasting achievement.

For now, focus on becoming a student of your child's unique motivation patterns. Notice what energizes them, what sustains their interest, and what helps them push through challenges. Trust in this process of discovery and alignment. You're not just helping your child manage ADHD; you're helping them unlock their natural potential for success.

Remember, the goal isn't perfection; it's progress. Each step toward understanding and working with your child's brain chemistry brings you closer to a learning environment where motivation flows more naturally and success feels within reach. The journey might look different than you expected, but the destination, a confident, capable learner, is absolutely achievable.

Chapter 3:

The Organization Revolution: Simple Systems for Academic Achievement

Organization isn't just about neat folders and color-coded notebooks; it's about creating systems that actually make sense to the ADHD brain. When we understand that traditional organizational methods often fail our children, not because they're lazy or unmotivated, but because these systems don't align with how their minds naturally work, we can begin to revolutionize their academic experience. "Sometimes the biggest act of courage is a small one." - Lauren Raffo

As a school counselor with decades of experience, I've witnessed firsthand how traditional organizational methods often set our ADHD children up for frustration and failure. The truth is, their brains process and organize information differently, requiring unique systems that work with their natural tendencies rather than against them.

Emma's desk used to look like a paper tornado had swept through it; assignments crumpled at the bottom of her backpack, important documents mixed with old lunch notes, and textbooks scattered everywhere. As her school counselor, I worked with Emma to develop what we called her "Command Center," a visual organization system that matched her brain's need for immediate visibility and quick access. Instead of forcing traditional filing systems, we created a large wall-mounted board with clear pockets for each subject, color-coded tabs for different types of assignments, and a prominent weekly calendar. The transformation wasn't just in her physical space; it was in her confidence. Within weeks, Emma went from constantly forgetting assignments to independently managing her workload. One afternoon, she burst into my office, beaming with pride, clutching a math test she'd remembered to study for using her new system. "Mrs. Adams," she exclaimed, "for the first time, I knew exactly where everything was, and I didn't panic!" This wasn't just about organization; it was about Emma discovering she could succeed when given tools that worked for her unique way of thinking.

In this chapter, we'll explore how to revolutionize your child's organizational system by creating structures that align with their natural thinking patterns. We'll dive into practical, visual organization methods that make sense to the ADHD brain, discover time management techniques that actually stick, and build sustainable homework systems that boost executive functioning rather than fight against it.

The key isn't forcing our children to adapt to systems that weren't designed for them; it's about creating new approaches that harness their strengths and support their challenges. By understanding how the ADHD brain processes information and manages tasks differently, we can transform daily struggles into opportunities for success.

Through practical strategies, visual tools, and step-by-step guidance, you'll learn how to help your child develop organizational skills that last beyond the school years. More importantly, you'll discover how to build these systems while preserving your child's confidence and nurturing their unique abilities.

Remember, organization isn't about perfection; it's about progress. As we explore these strategies together, keep in mind that what works for one child might need adjustment for another. The goal is to find and fine-tune approaches that resonate with your child's specific needs and natural tendencies.

Visual Organization Systems: Creating Clear Pathways to Success

Imagine walking into a store where everything is hidden behind opaque doors with tiny labels; frustrating, right? For children with ADHD, this is how traditional organizational systems often feel. The ADHD brain craves immediate visual access to information and materials,[26] which is why creating clear, visible pathways to success is crucial.

Let me share a transformative moment with one of my students, Maya. Her backpack was a black hole where assignments disappeared, and her desk looked like a paper explosion. Together, we created what we called her "Visual Command Station," a clear, accessible system that made organization nearly automatic.

Here are the key elements of effective visual organization that worked for Maya and countless other students:

- Clear containers that allow immediate visibility of contents
- Color-coding for different subjects or task types
- Visual schedules with pictures or icons

- Graphic organizers for breaking down complex information
- Task boards showing work status (To Do, In Progress, Complete)

The magic of visual organization lies in its simplicity and accessibility.[28] Think of it as creating a roadmap that your child's brain can naturally follow. When information is presented visually, it reduces the mental effort required to remember where things are and what needs to be done.

One particularly effective tool is the Visual Activity Schedule (VAS). Research shows these step-by-step visual guides significantly improve task completion rates and reduce off-task behavior.[27] For instance, Maya's morning routine transformed from a daily struggle into a smooth process when we created a simple visual checklist with pictures showing each step.

When implementing visual organization systems, consider these essential guidelines:

- Start small; implement one visual support at a time
- Involve your child in creating and personalizing their systems
- Use clear, consistent visual cues
- Make materials easily visible and accessible
- Regularly review and adjust what's working

Environmental organization plays a crucial role, too. Create designated zones for different activities, each with its own visual markers. A homework station might include clear supply containers, a visual timer, and a prominently displayed assignment checklist.

Remember, consistency is key when implementing these systems.[28] While classroom and home systems don't need to be identical, maintaining similar visual principles helps your child recognize and apply organizational strategies across different environments.

Pay attention to your child's natural tendencies.[29] Some children prefer digital tools with visual interfaces, while others respond better to physical charts and containers. The goal is to create systems that feel intuitive and supportive rather than imposed and restrictive.

One parent I worked with, Adele, transformed her daughter's study space using these principles. They created a "Weekly Launch Pad," a clear wall organizer with separate pockets for each day's materials, color-coded by subject. "For the first time," Adele told me, "my daughter can see exactly what she needs and where everything goes. It's like we finally found the right language for her brain."

Most importantly, celebrate progress along the way. Every successfully completed task, every item put in its proper place, and every routine followed is a step toward greater independence and confidence. These small victories build the foundation for long-term success.

Remember that perfect organization isn't the goal; functionality is. The best system is one that your child will actually use, one that makes their daily tasks easier rather than adding another layer of complexity to their day. When visual organization tools align with how your child's brain naturally works, what once seemed like insurmountable challenges become manageable steps toward success.

Time Management Through Brain-Friendly Routines

"Time isn't just about the clock; it's about how our brains process and navigate the moments of our day," I often tell parents who are struggling to help their children manage schedules and deadlines. For children with ADHD, traditional time management approaches often feel like trying to catch water with a net. Their brains process time differently,[33] requiring unique strategies that work with their natural rhythms rather than against them.

Let me share Jason's story. When he first came to my office, his parents were frustrated by his seeming inability to complete even simple tasks within reasonable timeframes. Instead of immediately implementing a rigid schedule, we took time to understand how Jason perceived time. We discovered that his ADHD brain needed more concrete, visual representations of time passing.

Here are the core strategies we developed that transformed Jason's relationship with time:

- Visual timers that make time tangible and visible
- Task chunking with built-in movement breaks
- Routines that incorporate novelty and choice
- Multi-sensory time markers (colors, sounds, physical cues)
- Body-doubling sessions for sustained focus

The key to successful time management isn't forcing ADHD brains to conform to traditional methods; it's creating systems that align with how they naturally process time and maintain attention.[31] We modified the classic Pomodoro Technique for Jason, using 15-minute work sessions followed by 5-minute movement breaks, perfectly matching his natural attention span while providing the physical activity his body craved.[26]

Consistency across environments proves crucial for lasting success. When parents and teachers jointly reinforce these routines, children develop a stronger sense of time management and control.[32] However, remember that consistency doesn't mean rigidity - the key is maintaining structure while allowing enough flexibility to keep engagement high.

Body doubling, working alongside someone else who is also focused on a task, became particularly powerful for Jason. Whether it was homework time with a parent nearby or virtual study sessions with friends, this social accountability provided the external motivation needed to maintain focus without creating pressure.[31]

Creating an environment that supports these routines is equally important. We helped Jason set up a dedicated study space with minimal distractions, clearly organized materials, and visual schedules. Color-coded folders, wall-mounted timers, and designated activity zones created external cues that supported his internal time management.[30]

Remember to start small when implementing new routines. Choose one or two strategies to begin with, allowing your child to develop comfort and confidence before adding more complexity. Celebrate the small wins; every completed task or smooth transition represents progress toward better time management skills.[30]

Encourage self-reflection by having your child participate in identifying what works best for them. Simple questions like "When do you feel most focused?" or "What helps you know how much time has passed?" can lead to valuable insights and ownership of their time management journey.

For instance, Jason discovered that using a sand timer for reading sessions helped him stay engaged better than a digital clock. This insight led us to incorporate more tactile time markers into his daily routines, significantly improving his ability to gauge time passing.

The goal isn't perfect adherence to a system but rather developing tools that help your child navigate time more effectively and confidently. When routines align with how the ADHD brain naturally works,[31] what once seemed impossible becomes not just manageable, but achievable.

Most importantly, maintain patience and flexibility as you help your child develop these skills. Time management may look different for ADHD brains, but with the right support and understanding, every child can learn to navigate their day successfully. Remember, we're not trying to fix their natural rhythms; we're creating systems that help them thrive within them.

The Homework Command Center: Building a Sustainable Study System

"A place for everything and everything in its place" takes on new meaning when designing study spaces for ADHD minds. Rather than forcing traditional organizational systems, let's create a command center that works with your child's natural tendencies while building sustainable habits for academic success.

In my years as a school counselor, I've seen countless students transform their academic experience through well-designed homework command centers. These aren't just organized spaces; they're carefully crafted environments that support focus, reduce overwhelm, and make success feel achievable.

Let's break down the essential components of an effective homework command center:

- A clearly designated workspace with minimal visual distractions
- An analog clock or visual timer within direct sight
- Supply stations with frequently-used items within arm's reach
- A vertical organization system for current assignments
- Color-coded folders or bins for different subjects
- A prominent monthly calendar for tracking due dates
- A daily checklist station for breaking down tasks

The key to success lies in personalization and simplicity. Over-complicated systems quickly become abandoned, while customized setups that match your child's preferences and needs have staying power. Think of it as creating a cockpit where everything necessary for success is within reach and visually accessible.

One particularly effective approach I've found is the "flow and accessibility" principle. Arrange items in the order they'll be used, from checking the calendar to grabbing supplies, creating a natural sequence that supports executive functioning. This reduces the mental energy spent on organization, leaving more cognitive resources for actual learning.

Consider Angeline, a seventh-grader who struggled with homework completion until we redesigned her study space. We created zones in her command center: a "launch pad" for reviewing assignments, a "work zone" with essential supplies, and a "completion station" for organizing finished work. The transformation wasn't just in her physical space; it was in her confidence and independence.

Sustainability is crucial for any organizational system, but especially for children with ADHD. The most beautiful command center won't help if it's not maintained. I recommend tying system check-ins to existing routines; perhaps during after-school snack time or as part of the evening routine. This creates natural accountability without adding another "to-do" to remember.

When setting up your command center, keep these key principles in mind:

- Keep it simple and intuitive
- Make everything visible and easily accessible
- Use color-coding and clear labels
- Group related items together
- Include space for both storage and active work

The power of a homework command center lies not just in its physical organization but in its ability to reduce anxiety and build confidence. When children know where to find what they need and can see their tasks clearly laid out, the overwhelming nature of homework becomes more manageable.

Regular review and adjustment are essential parts of maintaining an effective system. Schedule monthly check-ins with your child to discuss what's working and what needs tweaking. This collaborative approach not only improves the system but also helps develop valuable self-advocacy skills.

Remember, perfection isn't the goal; progress is. Your child's command center should evolve as their needs change and their executive function skills develop. What works in September might need adjustment by January, and that's perfectly okay. The key is creating a flexible foundation that supports your child's unique way of thinking and working.

I always remind parents that organizational systems are tools, not rules. The goal isn't to create a picture-perfect space but to build an environment where your child feels capable and supported. When we provide the right tools and structure, we empower our children to take control of their learning journey, one assignment at a time.

By implementing these strategies thoughtfully and consistently, you're not just organizing school supplies; you're building a framework for academic success that can grow with your child. The confidence and skills developed through managing their command center often extend far beyond homework time, supporting greater independence and success in all areas of life. "Organization isn't about being perfect; it's about building systems that work for your unique brain." - Dr. Russell Barkley

As we've explored throughout this chapter, revolutionizing organization for the ADHD brain isn't about forcing traditional methods or expecting perfection. It's about understanding and working with your child's natural tendencies to create systems that actually stick. Through visual organization strategies, brain-friendly time management, and personalized study spaces, we can transform daily struggles into opportunities for success.

Emma's journey from overwhelming chaos to confident self-management reminds us that when we align organizational tools with how the ADHD brain naturally works, we don't just create tidier spaces; we build confidence, independence, and a foundation for lasting academic achievement. Her transformation highlights the power of personalized, visual systems that make sense to the ADHD mind.

As you move forward with implementing these strategies, keep these essential principles in mind:

- Visual organization systems should be clear, accessible, and personally meaningful
- Time management works best when broken into brain-friendly chunks with regular movement breaks
- Study spaces thrive when designed around your child's natural tendencies and needs
- Progress matters more than perfection
- Flexibility and adaptability keep systems sustainable

Remember that organization is a skill that develops over time, not overnight. Each small victory, whether it's maintaining a homework command center for a week or remembering to check a visual schedule, builds momentum toward greater independence and confidence. Your role isn't to enforce rigid systems but to guide your child toward discovering what works best for their unique way of thinking.

The strategies we've discussed, from creating visual organization systems to establishing brain-friendly routines and building effective homework command centers, are more than just organizational tools. They're stepping stones toward self-sufficiency, academic success, and lasting confidence.

In our next chapter, we'll explore how to move beyond simple behavior management to teach lasting self-regulation skills. But first, take time to implement and adjust the organizational strategies we've discussed. Start with one approach that resonates most strongly with your child's needs and build from there. Remember, you're not just organizing papers and pencils; you're creating pathways for your child to thrive.

Most importantly, celebrate the progress along the way. Every organized folder, completed assignment, and followed routine represents a step toward greater independence. With patience, consistency, and the right tools, your child can develop organizational skills that support not just their academic success, but their confidence and capability in all areas of life.

Chapter 4:

Beyond Behavior: Teaching Self-Regulation Skills That Last

The morning sun streamed through my office window as I watched ten-year-old Matthew transform from a bundle of frustrated energy to a composed young problem-solver, simply by applying the "pause and plan" technique we'd been practicing. This moment crystallized what I'd learned over four decades of counseling: self-regulation isn't about controlling behavior; it's about teaching children to understand and navigate their own emotional landscape. "Understanding comes before change," my mentor often reminded me during my early counseling years. Those words echo through my experiences working with children who struggle with emotional regulation and self-control.

Over my four decades as a school counselor, I've witnessed countless bright, capable students grappling with the intense emotions that often accompany ADHD. Their parents frequently arrive in my office exhausted and discouraged, having tried every behavioral chart and consequence system available. What they often don't realize is that these traditional approaches miss a crucial truth: self-regulation isn't about controlling behavior; it's about understanding and working with the unique way the ADHD brain processes emotions.

Victoria's story perfectly illustrates this principle. Her journey from emotional overwhelm to measured self-awareness demonstrates how the right tools and understanding can transform daily struggles into opportunities for growth. Like many children with ADHD, Victoria's initial challenges weren't due to a lack of desire to succeed; her brain simply needed different strategies to process and manage intense emotions.

Victoria had always struggled with emotional outbursts during homework time, particularly when facing math problems. One afternoon, after a particularly challenging session where she'd torn up her worksheet in frustration, we sat down together to create what we called her "Calm Corner." We transformed a quiet space in her room with a soft beanbag chair, fidget tools, and a visual reminder of her three favorite calming strategies: deep dragon breaths, squeezing her stress ball, and counting backward from 20.

The real breakthrough came two weeks later when Victoria, feeling overwhelmed by a difficult problem, recognized her rising frustration before it peaked. Without prompting, she excused herself to her Calm Corner, spent five minutes using her tools, and returned ready to tackle the problem with renewed focus. This wasn't just about avoiding a meltdown; it was about Victoria developing the self-awareness and tools to regulate her emotions independently. That day, both Victoria and her parents realized that self-regulation wasn't about perfect behavior; it was about building skills that would serve her well beyond her school years.

In this chapter, we'll explore how to move beyond simple behavior management to develop lasting emotional control and self-awareness in children with ADHD. You'll learn practical strategies to help your child understand their emotional triggers, develop effective coping mechanisms, and build the resilience they need for long-term success.

Through tools like emotion wheels and guided scripts, you'll discover how to create an environment that supports emotional growth while honoring your child's unique way of experiencing the world.

Most importantly, you'll understand how anxiety and other emotional challenges often intertwine with ADHD, affecting your child's ability to regulate their responses. As we explore these connections, you'll gain insights into supporting your child through both everyday challenges and more complex emotional experiences.

Remember, the goal isn't to eliminate emotions; it's to help our children understand and manage them effectively. When we approach emotional regulation through this lens of understanding and support, we open the door to lasting positive change.

Understanding the ADHD Brain's Emotional Control Center

"The emotional brain responds to an event more quickly than the thinking brain." - Daniel Goleman

Imagine your child's brain as a bustling control room where emotions and thoughts constantly interact. In ADHD brains, this control room operates differently, creating unique challenges in emotional regulation. Through years of working with students like Matthew and Victoria, I've witnessed firsthand how understanding these differences can transform our approach to emotional support.[37]

Let's explore this control room using a practical tool I often share with families: the Emotion Wheel. Picture a colorful circle divided into basic emotions like joy, sadness, anger, and fear, with more nuanced feelings branching outward. This visual aid helps children identify and label their emotional experiences, making the abstract concrete. When children can name their feelings, they gain the first tool in managing them.[38]

The ADHD brain's emotional command center involves two key systems working in tandem, or sometimes, not so smoothly. The first is the limbic system, particularly the amygdala, which acts as an emotional alarm system. The second is the prefrontal cortex, which typically helps moderate these emotional responses. In children with ADHD, these systems don't communicate as effectively as they might in neurotypical brains.[37, 41]

This biological reality explains why your child might seem to react more intensely to situations than their peers. It's not about lack of control or willful behavior; it's about brain wiring. Studies have shown that children with ADHD often experience decreased activation in their prefrontal cortex, particularly in areas responsible for emotional regulation.[37, 38]

To help parents support their children through emotional challenges, I often share these practical phrases:

- "I see you're feeling strong emotions right now. Let's pause together."
- "What color would you give this feeling?"
- "Can you show me on the Emotion Wheel where you are right now?"

These simple scripts open doors to emotional awareness and provide a foundation for self-regulation. They acknowledge the intensity of feelings while creating space for reflection and response.[39]

The connection between ADHD and anxiety often intensifies emotional experiences. Many children with ADHD develop anxiety as a secondary challenge, creating a cycle where emotional responses become even more overwhelming. Understanding this connection helps us respond with greater compassion and targeted support.[40]

Remember Victoria's Calm Corner? This wasn't just about having a quiet space; it was about creating an environment that supported her brain's unique emotional processing needs. By incorporating visual aids, movement opportunities, and clear strategies, we helped her brain build stronger pathways for emotional regulation.[37, 38]

This knowledge transforms how we respond to emotional challenges. Instead of saying "calm down" or "control yourself," we can offer specific tools that work with their brain's natural tendencies. For instance, teaching deep breathing through "dragon breaths" or using movement to process emotions becomes more effective when we understand the neurological basis for these strategies.[39, 40]

The goal isn't to eliminate emotional responses; they're a vital part of human experience. Instead, we're working to help our children develop awareness and coping skills that match their brains' unique wiring. When we approach emotional regulation through this lens of understanding, we move from frustration to empowerment, from reaction to response.[41]

Building a Personal Regulation Toolkit: Strategies That Work

"Children develop self-regulation skills through experiencing co-regulation with supportive adults" - Dr. Stuart Shanker. This fundamental truth has guided my approach throughout decades of counseling, showing how adult modeling and support create the foundation for lasting emotional skills.

Let's explore practical strategies for building your child's regulation toolkit, focusing on tools that work with their natural tendencies rather than against them. Think of self-regulation like learning to ride a bike; you wouldn't expect a child to immediately pedal away without support. Instead, we provide training wheels, hold the back of the seat, and gradually release as they gain confidence.

One powerful starting point is the Emotion Wheel, a visual tool that helps children identify and label their feelings with greater precision. When children can name their emotions, they gain the first tool in managing them. Create a personalized version with your child, using colors and symbols that resonate with their experience.

Physical regulation strategies form another crucial component of the toolkit. Research shows that sensory activities can have an immediate impact on emotional balance. Here are some proven techniques:

- Deep pressure activities like bear hugs or weighted blankets
- Proprioceptive input through wall pushes or chair squeezes
- Vestibular movement using swinging or rocking
- Cold temperature sensation (like drinking ice water or holding a cold pack)

Breathing exercises become more effective when we make them concrete and engaging. Instead of simply saying "take deep breaths," try these child-friendly approaches:

- "Hot chocolate breath" - Hold an imaginary cup, smell deeply, blow to cool
- "Balloon belly" - Watch stomach rise and fall like a balloon
- "Dragon breaths" - Breathe fire out slowly with hands moving like flames

Task pairing is another essential strategy; combining regulation activities with challenging tasks. For example, create a pre-homework routine that includes physical movement and breathing exercises. This helps prepare your child's nervous system for focused attention.

Mindfulness doesn't need to mean sitting still (which can be particularly challenging for children with ADHD). Instead, focus on brief moments of awareness throughout the day:

- Taking three mindful breaths before starting homework
- Doing quick body scans during transition times
- Noticing five things they can see, hear, or touch

One often-overlooked strategy is the power of positive emotion. Research indicates that for children with ADHD, it's often more effective to up-regulate positive emotions than to try to down-regulate negative ones. Create opportunities for success by breaking tasks into manageable chunks and celebrating small wins.

Consistency is key when building these skills. Start small with one or two strategies that resonate with your child, and practice them regularly during calm moments. This builds the neural pathways needed for your child to access these tools during more challenging times.

Relationships and connection remain fundamental regulation tools. Spend time with your child doing activities they love, without correction or demands. This builds the emotional security that underlies all self-regulation skills.

Remember that anxiety often accompanies ADHD, intensifying emotional responses. Include specific anxiety-management techniques in your child's toolkit:

- Worry boxes for containing anxious thoughts
- Visualization exercises for feeling safe and calm
- Simple grounding techniques using the five senses

When implementing these strategies, think of yourself as a regulation coach rather than a behavior manager. Your role is to guide, support, and gradually help your child develop independence in using these tools. The goal isn't perfect behavior; it's building a toolkit of strategies your child can rely on throughout their life.

Most importantly, be patient with the process. Just as learning any new skill takes time and practice, developing regulation skills is a journey. Celebrate the small victories, learn from the setbacks, and keep building on what works for your unique child. With consistent support and the right tools, your child can develop the regulation skills they need to navigate life's challenges successfully.

From Meltdown to Mastery: Creating Supportive Environmental Systems

"The environment shapes behavior far more powerfully than willpower alone," I often remind parents who visit my office, drawing from decades of counseling experience. When we understand this fundamental truth, we can transform daily struggles into opportunities for growth and success.

Think of your child's environment as a dynamic support system rather than just a physical space. It's like creating a personal ecosystem that naturally encourages focus, emotional regulation, and successful task completion. Through my years of working with students, I've seen how thoughtfully designed environments can prevent meltdowns before they begin.

Let's explore the core elements of a supportive environment through the lens of the Emotion Wheel we discussed earlier. Each area of your child's space should address different emotional and functional needs:

- Calming Zone: A designated quiet space with soft textures, minimal visual stimulation, and comfort items
- Focus Zone: A well-organized workspace with clear visual systems and necessary tools within reach
- Movement Zone: An area that safely allows for physical activity and sensory input
- Reset Station: A structured space for transitions with visual schedules and grounding tools

The key is customization; what works for one child might overwhelm another. For instance, some children focus better with white noise, while others need complete quiet. Some benefit from fidget tools, while others find them distracting. Observation and collaboration with your child are essential in identifying their unique environmental needs.

Visual supports play a crucial role in creating predictability and reducing anxiety. Simple tools like visual schedules, emotion thermometers, and clearly labeled organization systems help make abstract concepts concrete. These aren't just organizational tools; they're anxiety management supports that help your child feel more in control of their environment.

Consider the story of Raymond, a student who struggled with homework meltdowns. We discovered that his after-school routine lacked clear environmental supports. Together, we created what he called his "Brain Station," a dedicated workspace with:

- A visual schedule showing his afternoon routine
- A timer that made time visible
- A "task map" breaking assignments into manageable chunks
- A collection of sensory tools for regulation breaks

Within weeks, Raymond's meltdowns decreased significantly. The environment was doing much of the heavy lifting, reducing the cognitive load required for transitions and task initiation.

Routines become more powerful when anchored in environmental supports. Create visual cues for transition times, establish clear placement for belongings, and maintain consistent locations for important activities. This environmental consistency reduces the executive function demands on your child's brain.

Importantly, these environmental supports should extend beyond home to school settings where possible. Work with teachers to implement similar strategies in the classroom. This consistency across environments helps solidify self-regulation skills and promotes independence.

Pay special attention to sensory considerations in the environment. Simple modifications can make a significant difference:

- Lighting: Reduce fluorescent glare or provide natural light options
- Sound: Offer noise-canceling headphones or create quiet zones
- Touch: Provide appropriate seating options and workspace textures
- Movement: Include opportunities for appropriate physical activity

Remember that environmental supports aren't about making things easier; they're about making success possible. Just as we use glasses to support vision or ramps to enable access, these environmental modifications help your child access their full potential.

As your child develops stronger self-regulation skills, you can gradually adjust these supports. Some children may need them long-term, while others might naturally fade certain supports as they develop independent strategies. The goal is to build confidence and competence through supported success.

When designing environmental supports, consider both immediate needs and long-term skill development. Each support should serve dual purposes: managing current challenges while building capacity for future independence. This balanced approach helps prevent dependence on supports while ensuring adequate assistance during skill development.

Most importantly, view environmental modifications as solutions rather than crutches. They're tools for success, just like any other learning aid. When we create environments that work with instead of against ADHD brains, we set the stage for lasting mastery and confident independence. "Every emotional challenge is an opportunity for growth." This truth has guided my work with countless children over four decades of counseling.

As we conclude our exploration of emotional regulation and self-awareness, let's reflect on the key principles we've uncovered. Throughout this chapter, we've seen how the ADHD brain processes emotions differently, requiring unique approaches to build lasting self-regulation skills. Victoria's journey with her Calm Corner showed us that success comes not from controlling emotions, but from understanding and working with them.

The science is clear: emotional regulation in ADHD isn't about willpower; it's about creating systems and environments that support your child's unique brain wiring. When we shift from trying to control behavior to supporting emotional development, we open the door to lasting positive change.

Remember these essential takeaways as you move forward:

- Understanding precedes regulation; help your child identify and label their emotions using tools like the Emotion Wheel
- Environment shapes behavior; create supportive spaces that promote calm and regulation

- Co-regulation leads to self-regulation; your consistent, compassionate presence matters
- Small wins build confidence; celebrate progress in emotional awareness and control
- Anxiety and ADHD often intertwine; address both for comprehensive support

Your role isn't to eliminate your child's emotional challenges; it's to guide them toward understanding and managing their emotional landscape effectively. With patience, consistency, and the right tools, your child can develop the self-regulation skills they need to thrive.

As Raymond demonstrated with his transformation from frustration to composed problem-solving, these skills develop gradually through supported practice. Each time your child successfully uses a regulation strategy or recognizes an emotional trigger, they're building neural pathways for future success.

In the next chapter, we'll explore how to create focus-friendly study routines that work with your child's natural tendencies rather than against them. But for now, remember that every step toward better emotional regulation, no matter how small, is a victory worth celebrating. You're not just helping your child manage today's challenges; you're building the foundation for lifelong emotional resilience and success.

Chapter 5:

The Homework Helper: Creating Focus-Friendly Study Routines

The kitchen table was covered in half-finished assignments, crumpled papers, and forgotten pencils; a scene all too familiar to parents of children with ADHD. But what if I told you that with the right environment and routines, homework time could become not just manageable, but actually productive? "Show me how a student does their homework, and I'll show you their path to academic success." - Maya Scott, Educational Psychologist

For many families, homework time has become the most dreaded part of the day. As I've witnessed countless times in my four decades as a school counselor, this daily struggle can leave both parents and children feeling defeated before they even begin. The good news? It doesn't have to be this way.

Hannah's story perfectly illustrates this transformation. When her mother first reached out to me in tears, their nightly homework battles often ended in meltdowns. Her daughter, a bright third-grader with ADHD, would spend hours at the kitchen table, distracted by every sound and movement in their busy household. During our first meeting, I helped them create a dedicated study space in Hannah's room; not a full desk setup, but a simple lap desk she could use while sitting on a therapy ball. We established a routine where Hannah would do 20 minutes of work followed by a 5-minute movement break, timing each session with a visual timer.

The transformation wasn't instant, but within weeks, Hannah's homework completion time had been cut in half. The real breakthrough came when Hannah proudly showed me her new 'homework success kit,' a clear pencil case with all her supplies, her visual timer, and a checklist she'd created herself. 'I'm not fighting my brain anymore,' she told me with a smile. 'I'm working with it.' This simple shift in environment and routine had turned their evening battles into productive study sessions, proving that sometimes the smallest changes can make the biggest difference.

In this chapter, we'll explore how to create these transformative changes in your own home. You'll discover practical strategies for setting up focus-friendly study spaces, implementing effective break schedules, and developing routines that work with, not against, your child's ADHD brain. We'll examine how to break down assignments into manageable chunks, use timing techniques that boost concentration, and create organization systems that stick.

Most importantly, you'll learn how to shift homework time from a source of stress to an opportunity for growth and success. Because when we understand how to support our children's unique learning needs, we can help them develop the skills and confidence they need to thrive academically, not just today, but throughout their educational journey.

Creating the Optimal Study Environment: Setting Up Spaces That Support Focus

"Creating the ideal environment is like setting the stage for a great performance; when everything is in place, success becomes much more achievable." - Dr. Sarah Chen, Educational Neuropsychologist.

When it comes to helping children with ADHD focus on schoolwork, the physical space where they study matters more than most parents realize.[46, 47, 48] Research consistently shows that environmental factors can significantly impact concentration, retention, and overall academic performance, especially for ADHD brains that are naturally more sensitive to their surroundings.

Let's explore how to create a study sanctuary that works with your child's unique needs, breaking down the essential elements that support focus and learning:

- Light and Visual Environment
- Position the study area to maximize natural daylight when possible
- Use adjustable task lighting to reduce eye strain and maintain alertness
- Create a visual buffer from distracting views or activities
- Consider using a study carrel or portable screen for extra focus during intense work

The right lighting can make a dramatic difference in how long your child maintains attention. Amy, a student I worked with, went from 15-minute focus spans to nearly an hour simply by moving her desk near a window and adding a desk lamp with adjustable brightness.

Sound Strategy

While complete silence works for some children, many with ADHD actually focus better with some background sound.[48, 31] Consider testing different audio environments:

- White noise machines or nature sound apps
- Instrumental music (avoiding songs with lyrics)
- Noise-canceling headphones for blocking disruptive sounds
- Consistent, gentle background sounds like a small fan

Work with your child to find their optimal sound environment through trial and error. What works during reading might differ from what helps during math practice.

Movement-Friendly Seating

The ADHD brain often thinks better when the body can move.[46, 49] Create a workspace that allows for:

- Active seating options like wobble stools or therapy balls
- Standing desk alternatives for movement while working
- Fidget tools that don't distract from schoolwork
- Comfortable but supportive seating that maintains good posture

I've seen remarkable improvements in focus when children are permitted to move while learning. One student doubled his homework completion rate simply by switching from a traditional chair to a wobble stool.

Organization That Makes Sense

Clutter is particularly challenging for the ADHD brain.[46, 48] Design a study space with:

- Clear containers for frequently used supplies
- Visual organizers and labeled storage solutions
- A designated spot for completed work
- Only essential items on the work surface
- Color-coding systems for different subjects

The key is maintaining organization without creating visual overwhelm. Consider using closed storage for items not immediately needed.

Sensory Considerations

Children with ADHD often have heightened sensory awareness.[47] Pay attention to:

- Room temperature control
- Air quality and ventilation
- Comfortable textures in seating and work surfaces
- Minimal visual distractions on walls
- Proper ergonomics for reducing physical strain

Technology Management

In today's digital world, managing tech distractions is crucial.[31] Structure the space to:

- Keep phones out of sight during work time
- Position screens away from high-traffic areas
- Use website blockers during study hours
- Create separate zones for digital and non-digital work

Location Strategy

Choose a study spot that's:

- Away from high-traffic areas but not isolated
- Close enough for parent support when needed
- Separate from play and relaxation spaces
- Consistent; using the same space builds routine[47, 48]

Remember, the perfect study environment looks different for every child. Start with these foundational elements and adjust based on your child's responses and preferences. Sometimes small changes, like adding a fidget tool[47, 49] or adjusting lighting, can make a significant difference in focus and productivity.

Most importantly, involve your child in setting up their study space. When children have input into their environment, they're more likely to feel ownership and use the space effectively. Ask them what helps them focus best and be open to making adjustments as their needs change.

One parent I worked with created a "focus station" with her daughter, complete with a special lamp they chose together and a customized organization system using her favorite colors. This collaborative approach not only resulted in a more effective study space but also strengthened their relationship and her daughter's commitment to using it.

The right study environment won't eliminate all ADHD challenges, but it can significantly reduce unnecessary struggles and set your child up for greater academic success.[46, 47, 48] Think of it as creating a launch pad; the right conditions make lift-off much easier.

The Power of Structured Breaks: Using Time Management Techniques That Work With ADHD Brains

"Time management isn't about squeezing more into every minute; it's about making every minute count through strategic rest and renewal."
- Dr. Russell Barkley, ADHD Expert

Imagine trying to sprint a marathon. Sounds impossible, right? Yet this is exactly what we ask of our children with ADHD when we expect them to maintain focus for long stretches without breaks. Research consistently shows that children with ADHD experience time differently than their neurotypical peers; their internal clock often runs faster, making sustained attention feel like an uphill battle.[53]

The good news? Strategic breaks aren't just helpful; they're scientifically proven to enhance focus, reduce mental fatigue, and improve overall productivity.[50] Let's explore how to make breaks work for, not against, the ADHD brain.

The Magic of Movement Breaks:

- Quick stretching or yoga pose
- Walking or marching in place
- Simple jumping jacks or dance moves
- Balance exercise
- Deep breathing combined with movement

Think of these breaks as your child's mental reset button. Research shows that physical activity during breaks helps dissipate restlessness and refreshes the mind more effectively than passive activities like screen time.[50]

Timing is everything when it comes to structured breaks. For most children with ADHD, the sweet spot tends to be:

- 10-15 minutes of focused work for younger children
- 15-20 minutes for older elementary students
- 20-25 minutes for middle school and above
- 5-minute breaks between work sessions

But remember, these aren't rigid rules; they're starting points. Pay attention to your child's natural rhythm and adjust accordingly. Some students might need shorter work periods with more frequent breaks, while others might surprise you with their ability to focus for longer stretches once they trust that breaks are coming.[50]

One powerful approach is the modified Pomodoro Technique for ADHD brains.[51] This method uses visual timers to make time concrete and visible, breaking work into manageable chunks with strategic movement breaks. The key lies in making both work periods and breaks predictable and structured.

Here's what effective break structuring looks like in practice:

- Set clear start and end times using visual timers
- Define specific break activities in advance
- Keep breaks active but not overwhelming
- Avoid screens during a short break
- Return to work promptly when the break ends

I've seen this approach transform homework battles into productive study sessions. Take Maya, a middle school student who struggled with lengthy assignments. We implemented a "25/5" pattern, 25 minutes of focused work followed by 5-minute movement breaks. Her mother reported that homework completion time dropped by half, while the quality of her work actually improved.

One common concern I hear from parents is that breaks will disrupt their child's concentration or make it harder to get back to work. However, research consistently shows the opposite is true for ADHD brains.[52] Regular, structured breaks actually improve focus, reduce resistance to tasks, and help maintain consistent energy levels throughout homework time.

Think of it like interval training for the brain. Just as athletes use structured intervals to build endurance, children with ADHD can use strategic breaks to build their focusing muscles. The goal isn't to eliminate the need for breaks but to use them effectively as tools for success.

Remember, implementing structured breaks isn't about giving in to distraction; it's about working with your child's natural brain wiring to optimize learning and reduce frustration. When we honor the ADHD brain's need for regular renewal, we create an environment where sustained attention becomes possible and productivity can flourish.

The beauty of this approach lies in its simplicity and flexibility. You don't need special equipment or extensive training; just an understanding of your child's needs and a willingness to structure time in a way that supports their success. Start small, be consistent, and watch as breaks transform from battle grounds into bridges to better focus and learning.

From Overwhelm to Action: Breaking Down Assignments into Manageable Steps

"The difference between overwhelm and progress often comes down to how we frame the task in front of us." - Dr. Russell Barkley

Let's be honest; there's nothing quite like watching your child spiral into overwhelm when faced with a complex assignment. That blank stare, the tears of frustration, or the immediate "I can't do this!" It's heartbreaking, and as parents, our instinct is to jump in and rescue them. But what if I told you there's a better way?

The ADHD brain processes large tasks differently from neurotypical brains. When faced with a multi-step assignment, children with ADHD often experience what experts call "task paralysis," a state where the magnitude of the work ahead feels so overwhelming that starting seems impossible. This isn't laziness or defiance; it's their executive functioning challenges, making it difficult to break down big projects into manageable pieces.[54, 57]

Let me introduce you to the B.R.E.A.K. method, a system I've developed over decades of working with ADHD students:

- Begin with a brain dump
- Rank tasks by priority
- Estimate time needed
- Arrange into chunks
- Keep track visually

This method works because it makes the invisible visible. Children with ADHD need concrete, visual representations of abstract concepts like time and task sequence.[57] Think of it like building with LEGOs; you wouldn't hand a child a picture of the finished product and expect them to figure it out. You'd give them step-by-step instructions with clear pictures for each stage.

Here's how to put this into practice:

- Use a large whiteboard or paper to list every component of the assignment
- Help your child estimate realistic time frames for each piece
- Break large chunks into 15-20 minute tasks
- Create visual checkpoints for progress
- Celebrate each completed step

One particularly effective strategy is the "5-Minute Start." When a child feels overwhelmed, have them commit to working on just one small piece for five minutes. This breaks through the paralysis of perfectionism and gets momentum flowing. Often, once started, children will naturally continue beyond the five-minute mark.[57]

Tools that can help:

- Visual timers to make time concrete
- Sticky notes for movable task lists
- Color-coding systems for different types of work
- Checklists with specific, actionable steps
- Progress trackers to celebrate small wins

I recently worked with a student named James who struggled with writing assignments. Instead of staring at a blank page, we broke his essay into tiny tasks; each paragraph became its own mission, with clear checkpoints along the way. We used different colored sticky notes for each section, making the process visual and tactile. Within weeks, James went from avoiding writing assignments to tackling them with confidence, all because we made the invisible steps visible.

Remember, the goal isn't perfection; it's progress. Research shows that children with ADHD are more likely to complete tasks successfully when they can see clear, concrete steps and understand exactly what's expected at each stage.[54, 58]

The most important thing to remember is that overwhelm is not a character flaw; it's a very real response to executive functioning challenges.[54, 57] By providing structure and breaking down assignments into bite-sized pieces, we're not just helping our children complete their work; we're teaching them valuable skills they'll use throughout their lives.

When we shift our approach from "Why can't you just get started?" to "Let's figure out the first small step together," we change the entire dynamic.[54] We move from frustration to partnership, from overwhelm to action, one manageable step at a time.

Every major project that's ever been completed, from building skyscrapers to writing novels, started with a single small action. By teaching our children how to break down big tasks into manageable steps, we're not just helping them with today's homework; we're equipping them with skills that will serve them well into adulthood.[54,]

[55, 56, 57, 58] "Success isn't about perfection; it's about progress, one manageable step at a time." - Dr. Russell Barkley

As we conclude our exploration of homework strategies, remember that transforming study time from a battle into a foundation for success is an ongoing journey. The key lies in creating systems that work with your child's unique ADHD brain, not against it.

Through this chapter, we've discovered how thoughtfully designed study spaces, strategic breaks, and breaking down overwhelming tasks can revolutionize homework time. These aren't just techniques; they're bridges to independence and academic confidence.

What stands out most from Hannah's story isn't just her improved homework completion; it's how she took ownership of her learning process. When she proudly showed me her self-created homework success kit, complete with a visual timer and personalized checklist, she demonstrated something profound: given the right tools and understanding, children with ADHD can develop their own strategies for success.

As you implement changes in your own home, keep these essential takeaways in mind:

- The environment shapes behavior more than willpower ever could
- Strategic breaks aren't interruptions; they're vital tools for sustained focus
- Breaking down assignments isn't hand-holding; it's teaching essential life skills
- Visual systems make the invisible visible and the overwhelming manageable

- Success looks different for every child; celebrate progress, not perfection

Remember to stay flexible and patient. What works brilliantly one week might need tweaking the next. That's not failure; it's part of the process of finding what truly works for your child. The goal isn't to eliminate ADHD challenges but to build a toolkit of strategies that make them manageable.

Your role in this journey is crucial, but remember, you're not just helping with homework. You're teaching valuable executive functioning skills that will serve your child well beyond their school years. Every organized workspace, every well-timed break, every broken-down task is an investment in their future independence.

In the next chapter, we'll explore how to advocate effectively for your child at school, ensuring these homework strategies align with classroom support. But for now, focus on implementing one small change at a time. Remember, just as Rome wasn't built in a day, transforming homework habits takes time, consistency, and compassion, both for your child and yourself.

Start where you are, celebrate small wins, and trust that with the right support and strategies, your child can develop the skills they need to tackle homework successfully. After all, it's not about creating perfect students; it's about empowering capable learners who understand how to work with their unique brains.

Chapter 6:

Classroom Champions: Advocating for Your Child at School

The difference between a struggling student and a thriving learner often comes down to having the right support system in place at school. As your child's primary advocate, you hold the power to help shape their educational experience by understanding their rights, communicating effectively with school staff, and ensuring appropriate accommodations are not just promised but properly implemented. "Success comes not from having the perfect plan, but from having the courage to speak up and take action," notes Dr. Sarah Thompson, a respected educational advocate whose wisdom has guided countless families through their advocacy journey.

As both a parent and long-time school counselor, I've witnessed how critical advocacy skills become in shaping a child's educational journey. During my third decade as a school counselor, I worked with a student named Bonnie who perfectly illustrated this truth. Bonnie was struggling to keep up in her advanced math class despite having a brilliant mind for numbers. Her ADHD made it difficult to process multiple-step problems in the traditional format her teacher used. After observing Bonnie's frustration, I collaborated with her parents to advocate for a simple yet effective accommodation: allowing her to use a step-by-step checklist and graph paper to organize complex problems.

We scheduled a meeting with her math teacher, bringing not just the challenge but a concrete solution to the table. The teacher was initially hesitant, worried about fairness to other students, but we explained how this accommodation wouldn't give Bonnie an advantage; it would simply allow her to demonstrate her true capabilities. Within weeks of implementing this change, Bonnie's test scores rose from C's to A's, and more importantly, her confidence soared. This experience perfectly illustrates how targeted advocacy, combined with practical solutions, can transform a child's academic experience.

As we dive into this chapter, you'll discover that effective advocacy isn't about confrontation; it's about collaboration. It's about understanding your child's rights, yes, but also about building bridges with educators who often want to help but may not know how. You'll learn practical strategies for communicating your child's needs, documenting important interactions, and ensuring that support plans don't just exist on paper but translate into real classroom success.

Remember, you are your child's most important advocate, and your voice matters. Whether you're navigating IEP meetings, discussing accommodations with teachers, or working to create a more supportive classroom environment, the skills and strategies in this chapter will help you become a more confident and effective champion for your child's education.

Understanding and Securing Educational Rights: IEPs, 504 Plans, and Legal Protections

"The difference between struggling and thriving at school often comes down to having the right support systems in place," shares Maria Chen, whose daughter transformed from a frustrated learner to a confident student after securing appropriate educational accommodations. As a school counselor, I've seen firsthand how understanding and effectively utilizing educational rights can open doors for students with ADHD.

Navigating educational rights may feel overwhelming at first, but breaking it down into manageable pieces makes it more approachable. There are two primary legal frameworks designed to support students with ADHD: Individualized Education Programs (IEPs) and 504 Plans.[62] Let's explore each to help you determine which path might best serve your child's needs.

IEPs fall under the Individuals with Disabilities Education Act (IDEA)[62] and provide comprehensive support when ADHD significantly impairs educational performance and requires specialized instruction.[61] To qualify, your child's ADHD must demonstrate limited alertness that adversely affects their educational performance under the category of "Other Health Impaired."[61] Think of an IEP as a detailed roadmap, complete with specialized instruction, related services, and specific accommodations tailored to your child's unique needs.[61, 62]

504 Plans, stemming from Section 504 of the Rehabilitation Act of 1973,[62] often prove more accessible for many students with ADHD as they don't require the same level of impairment as an IEP.[62] If your child's ADHD substantially limits major life activities like concentrating or thinking, they may qualify for a 504 Plan.[62] These plans focus on providing accommodations that level the playing field, such as extended time for tests or reduced-distraction environments.[60]

MEETING PREPARATION CHECKLIST:

- Gather recent progress reports and report cards
- Document specific challenges your child faces in school
- List current strategies that work at home
- Prepare specific questions about available accommodations
- Bring any private evaluations or medical documentation
- Consider bringing a supportive friend or advocate

The evaluation process deserves careful attention. Whether pursuing an IEP or 504 Plan, you have the right to request an evaluation from your school district.[62] This evaluation should be comprehensive, considering multiple sources of information, including teacher observations, academic performance, and any private evaluations.[62]

SAMPLE EMAIL TEMPLATE FOR REQUESTING EVALUATION:

Subject: Request for Educational Evaluation

"Dear [Administrator's Name],

I am writing to formally request a comprehensive educational evaluation for my child, [Child's Name], who is currently in [Teacher's Name]'s [Grade] class. [Child's Name] has been diagnosed with ADHD and is experiencing significant challenges with [specific challenges]. I believe [he/she] may need additional support to access the curriculum effectively.

Please provide me with any necessary consent forms and information about the evaluation process. I look forward to working together to support [Child's Name]'s educational needs.

Best regards,
[Your Name]"

When it comes to advocating for your child, documentation becomes your strongest ally. Create a dedicated folder (physical or digital) for:

- All communications with the school
- Meeting notes and evaluation results
- Medical records and private evaluations
- Samples of schoolwork showing areas of concern
- Records of any incidents or challenges

COLLABORATION PROMPTS FOR TEACHER MEETINGS:

- "Can you help me understand how [specific challenge] presents in the classroom?"
- "What strategies have you found effective with my child?"
- "How can we work together to implement these accommodations?"
- "What's the best way to stay in touch about progress?"

Remember that these plans aren't set in stone; they should evolve with your child's needs. IEPs require annual reviews at a minimum, while 504 Plans should be reviewed periodically.[62] You have the right to request reviews more frequently if needed, and it's often beneficial to do so as your child's needs change.

If disagreements arise about your child's educational support, you have legal rights to challenge decisions.[61, 62] This might include requesting an independent evaluation or filing a formal complaint. However, approaching these situations collaboratively often yields better results than immediate confrontation. Most educators want to help; they sometimes just need guidance on how best to support your child.

Common accommodations that often prove beneficial for students with ADHD include:

- Extended time for tests and assignments[59, 60]
- Strategic seating arrangements[60]
- Break periods during instruction[59]
- Use of organizational tools and technology[59]
- Modified homework loads[60]
- Quiet testing environments[60]

The key to successful advocacy lies in approaching it as a partnership. Come to meetings prepared but open-minded, focusing on solutions rather than problems. Share your insights about what works at home, and be receptive to teachers' perspectives about classroom dynamics. Together, you can create a support system that helps your child thrive.

A parent I worked with had a daughter who struggled with time management. Instead of demanding immediate accommodations, she approached her daughter's teacher with curiosity and collaboration. "What strategies have you seen work for other students?" she asked. This opening created a productive dialogue that led to implementing a discrete timer system that benefited not just her daughter, but several other students as well.

Securing educational rights isn't a one-time achievement; it's an ongoing process of ensuring your child receives the support they need to succeed. Stay informed, stay organized, and most importantly, stay committed to being your child's most effective advocate. With the right support system in place, your child can develop both the skills and confidence needed to thrive in their educational journey.

Building Collaborative Partnerships with Teachers and School Staff

"The strongest partnerships are built on trust, understanding, and a shared commitment to student success," notes Dr. Rachel Martinez, Educational Psychologist and ADHD specialist. As we explore building effective partnerships with your child's teachers and school staff, remember that successful collaboration isn't just about attending parent-teacher conferences; it's about creating meaningful connections that support your child throughout the entire school year.

SAMPLE EMAIL TEMPLATE FOR TEACHER COMMUNICATION:

Subject: Opening Communication for [Student Name]

"Dear [Teacher's Name],

I hope your school year is off to a great start. I'm [Child's Name]'s parent, and I wanted to reach out early to establish open communication. [Child's Name] has ADHD, and I've found that certain strategies help [him/her] succeed in the classroom. Would you be open to a brief meeting to discuss what works best for [Child's Name] and hear your observations?

Best regards,
[Your Name]"

Let's get real for a minute; teachers are often juggling 20-30 students with diverse needs, and while they want to help your child succeed, they may not always have specialized training in ADHD. This is where your role as both parent and partner becomes crucial. You bring invaluable insights about your child's unique needs, challenges, and strengths that can help educators create more effective support strategies.

MEETING PREPARATION CHECKLIST:

- Prepare specific examples of successful strategies used at home
- Bring a brief summary of your child's ADHD profile
- List any current medications and their timing
- Note your child's strengths and interests
- Have specific questions ready about classroom routines
- Bring a notebook for taking notes

When initiating partnerships with school staff, timing matters. Schedule an early meeting before academic challenges arise. This proactive approach allows you to establish rapport and create support systems when stress levels are low. During these initial conversations, focus on learning about classroom routines and sharing specific examples of strategies that work at home.

COLLABORATION PROMPTS FOR PRODUCTIVE CONVERSATIONS:

- "What's the best way to stay in touch about [Child's Name]'s progress?"
- "How can I support your classroom strategies at home?"

- "What behaviors should trigger communication from either of us?"
- "How would you prefer to receive information about medication changes?"
- "What's the best time to reach you with questions?"

One particularly effective approach is to establish regular check-in routines. This might mean brief weekly email updates, monthly progress meetings, or using a shared communication log. The key is finding a sustainable system that works for both you and the teaching team.

I remember working with Trevor's mother, who transformed a challenging situation through thoughtful collaboration. Instead of expressing frustration about assignments being lost, she asked the teacher, "Could we brainstorm ways to make the homework turn-in process more consistent?" This opened a productive dialogue that led to implementing a simple but effective system using colored folders.

When sharing information about your child, focus on actionable insights. For example, instead of simply stating that your child has difficulty with transitions, explain that using a visual timer and five-minute warnings helps them prepare for activity changes. This kind of specific, solution-oriented information gives teachers practical tools they can implement in the classroom.

It's also important to recognize that teachers may have different perspectives on your child's behavior and needs. This isn't necessarily a bad thing; sometimes these varying viewpoints can lead to valuable insights and creative solutions. The goal is to bridge these perspectives to create a more complete understanding of your child's needs.

Don't forget to include other key school staff in your collaboration efforts. School counselors, special education teachers, and administrators can all play vital roles in supporting your child's success. Building relationships with these team members can provide additional advocacy and support channels.

When challenges arise, and they likely will, approach them as opportunities for problem-solving rather than conflicts. If a teacher expresses concern about your child's behavior, respond with "Let's work together to understand what's triggering this and find some solutions" rather than becoming defensive.

Remember that documentation is crucial. Keep a record of all communications, meetings, and agreed-upon strategies. This helps ensure consistency and provides a reference point for what's working and what needs adjustment. A simple shared Google Doc or email thread can work wonders for keeping everyone on the same page.

Finally, celebrate successes together, no matter how small. When a strategy works well or your child makes progress, share that positive feedback with the teaching team. This reinforces the value of your collaboration and helps maintain momentum for continued support.

By approaching school partnerships with intention, respect, and a solution-focused mindset, you create an environment where your child can thrive. Remember, you're not just advocating for your child; you're helping build a support system that can make a lasting difference in their educational journey.

Essential Classroom Accommodations and Modifications That Actually Work

"The right accommodations aren't about giving unfair advantages; they're about removing barriers so every child can show their true potential," reflects Maria Gonzalez, whose daughter transformed from a struggling student to an honor roll achiever after receiving appropriate classroom support.

As both a school counselor and advocate for students with ADHD, I've seen firsthand how the right accommodations can completely transform a child's learning experience. Take Jacob, whose grades jumped from D's to B's simply by implementing strategic seating and assignment modifications. His mother tearfully shared, "For the first time, my brilliant son can actually show what he knows."

Let's break down the most effective classroom accommodations into three key areas: environmental supports, instructional modifications, and assessment adjustments. Each category offers evidence-backed strategies that can dramatically improve learning outcomes.

Environmental Supports:

- Strategic seating near the teacher and away from distractions[67]
- Flexible seating options (wiggle cushions, standing desks)[49]
- Designated quiet work spaces for independent tasks[66]
- Visual schedules and timers to support transitions[49]
- Organized, clutter-free workspaces[67]

These environmental modifications help manage sensory input and support executive functioning. For instance, when we moved Sally's desk away from the window and provided a wobble stool, her ability to focus during lessons improved dramatically. The key is customizing these supports to match your child's specific needs.

Instructional Modifications:

- Breaking down complex assignments into smaller steps[66]
- Providing written instructions alongside verbal ones[67]
- Using multi-modal teaching approaches (visual, auditory, kinesthetic)[49]
- Incorporating movement breaks during lessons[66]
- Offering choice in assignment formats[67]

I worked with a teacher who transformed her approach for students with ADHD by creating what we called "task maps," visual breakdowns of assignment steps with clear checkpoints. This simple modification helped students maintain momentum and reduce overwhelm.

Assessment Accommodations

- Extended time for tests and assignments[66]
- Quiet testing environments[6]
- Alternative assessment formats[49]
- Breaking tests into smaller sections[66]
- Use of technology for written work[67]

When discussing accommodations with teachers, focus on specific challenges rather than broad diagnoses. Instead of saying "My child has ADHD and needs help," try "I've noticed they struggle with writing down assignments accurately. Could we explore using a digital planner?"

SAMPLE ACCOMMODATION REQUEST:
"Dear [Teacher's Name],

I've observed that [Child's Name] has difficulty completing multi-step math problems, though they understand the concepts. Could we discuss implementing a step-by-step checklist system? I've seen this work effectively at home and would be happy to share our approach.

Best regards,
[Your Name]"

Remember that accommodations should be reviewed and adjusted regularly. What works in September might need tweaking by January. Stay in communication with teachers about your child's progress and be open to trying new strategies.

MONITORING EFFECTIVENESS CHECKLIST:

- Track assignment completion rates
- Note changes in test scores
- Observe homework stress levels
- Monitor classroom participation
- Document organizational improvements

One particularly effective approach combines multiple accommodations to create a comprehensive support system. For example, a student might use a combination of preferential seating, a visual schedule, and assignment chunking to maximize their learning potential.

The key to successful accommodations lies in their implementation. Even the best-designed supports won't help if they're not consistently used or if your child feels embarrassed about using them. Work with teachers to ensure accommodations are provided discreetly and presented as tools for success rather than crutches.

I remember working with a middle school student named Alex who initially refused to use his accommodations because he felt they made him "different." We reframed the conversation, comparing his accommodations to a tennis player's choice of racket; they were simply tools that helped him perform his best. This shift in perspective helped him embrace the supports that ultimately led to significant academic improvement.

Finally, celebrate the successes these accommodations bring, no matter how small. Each completed assignment, each day of organized materials, each test taken without time pressure; these are victories that build confidence and create positive momentum for future learning.

Remember, effective accommodations aren't about making things easier; they're about making learning accessible. When we remove unnecessary barriers and provide appropriate support, we allow students with ADHD to demonstrate their true capabilities and build the confidence they need to succeed. "The greatest advocates aren't just the loudest voices; they're the ones who build bridges, create understanding, and never stop believing in their child's potential." - Dr. Sarah Thompson

As we conclude this chapter on advocacy, I'm reminded of Bonnie's story and how a simple accommodation, thoughtfully implemented through collaborative partnership, transformed not just her grades but her entire relationship with learning. Your journey as an advocate may sometimes feel overwhelming, but remember that the most powerful changes often begin with a single conversation.

We've explored the vital importance of understanding your child's educational rights; not just as legal protections, but as tools for creating meaningful change. Through our deep dive into IEPs, 504 plans, and essential accommodations, you've gained the foundation needed to advocate effectively. But perhaps more importantly, you've discovered that true advocacy is about building relationships and approaching teachers and school staff not as adversaries, but as potential allies in your child's success journey.

Remember, effective advocacy isn't a one-time event; it's an ongoing process of observation, communication, and adjustment. Your role as your child's advocate may feel daunting at times, but you're now equipped with practical strategies for:

- Building strong partnerships with educators
- Securing and implementing effective accommodations
- Documenting progress and challenges
- Maintaining productive communication channels
- Ensuring support plans are actually implemented

As you move forward, keep in mind that every small victory, whether it's a teacher implementing a new accommodation or your child feeling more confident in class, is worth celebrating. These wins build momentum for bigger changes and remind us that positive transformation is possible.

You've learned how to navigate the educational system, communicate effectively with school staff, and ensure your child receives the support they need to thrive. Remember that you don't have to do this alone. By building collaborative partnerships and understanding the resources available, you're creating a network of support that can make a real difference in your child's educational journey.

Your voice matters. Your insights about your child are invaluable. And with the tools and strategies we've explored in this chapter, you're well-equipped to be the advocate your child needs. Keep pushing forward, stay focused on solutions rather than problems, and never underestimate the power of persistent, positive advocacy.

As we move into the next chapter on family dynamics, carry with you the confidence that comes from knowing you can effectively champion your child's educational needs. After all, the most powerful force in transforming a child's academic experience isn't a perfect plan or policy; it's a parent who never stops believing in their child's potential and has the tools to turn that belief into action.

Chapter 7:

Family Harmony: Balancing ADHD Needs with Sibling Support

The ripple effects of ADHD extend far beyond the diagnosed child, touching every member of the family in unique and sometimes challenging ways. Creating harmony in a household where one child has ADHD requires thoughtful navigation, clear communication, and intentional effort to ensure every family member feels seen, heard, and valued. "When one child in a family has different needs, it affects the whole family dynamic; but this challenge can become an opportunity for everyone to grow stronger together." - Anonymous

Navigating family life with ADHD requires a delicate balance of attention, understanding, and strategic planning that encompasses every family member's needs. Often, parents find themselves caught in what feels like an impossible situation; trying to provide the extra support their ADHD child requires while ensuring their other children don't feel overlooked or less important.

During my years as a school counselor, I worked with a family I'll never forget. Willa, a bright-eyed third grader with ADHD, had two siblings who were struggling to understand why their sister seemed to get "special treatment." Their mother came to me in tears, explaining how her other children had started acting out and expressing feelings of being overlooked. Together, we developed a "family spotlight" system where each child had designated one-on-one time with parents and specific responsibilities that made them feel valued. For Willa's siblings, understanding that their sister's different needs weren't preferential treatment but necessary support was a game-changer. The turning point came when the family started having weekly "appreciation circles," where each child shared something they admired about their siblings. Over time, what began as a challenge transformed into a beautiful opportunity for the whole family to grow closer and more understanding of each other's unique qualities and needs.

This chapter will explore practical strategies for creating harmony in homes where ADHD is part of the family dynamic. We'll discuss how to address sibling resentment, establish fair family systems, and build stronger bonds between siblings. You'll learn how to help your non-ADHD children understand their siblings' challenges while ensuring they feel equally valued and supported.

The goal isn't to achieve perfect balance - that's an unrealistic expectation that can create more stress than solutions. Instead, we'll focus on creating an environment where every family member feels heard, understood, and appreciated for their unique contributions to the family unit. Through thoughtful communication, intentional family practices, and strategic planning, you can transform potential family tensions into opportunities for growth and deeper connection.

As we explore these strategies, remember that every family's journey is unique. The solutions that work for one family might need adjustment for another. What matters most is maintaining open dialogue, showing consistent love and attention to all your children, and creating systems that acknowledge and support everyone's needs.

Understanding and Addressing Sibling Emotions: From Resentment to Empathy

"When one child seems to get all the attention, it creates ripples through the whole family," shared Maria, mother of three, during a parent workshop. "My other kids started wondering if they needed to act out just to be noticed." This common sentiment echoes through many families navigating the complex dynamics of ADHD.

Siblings of children with ADHD often experience a complex mix of emotions, from frustration and jealousy to genuine concern and protectiveness. These feelings aren't just passing phases; they're valid responses to a family dynamic that can sometimes feel unbalanced. Understanding and addressing these emotions early is crucial for maintaining healthy family relationships.

One effective approach is creating structured opportunities for emotional expression. Consider implementing regular "feelings check-ins" where each sibling has dedicated time to share their thoughts and experiences. These sessions might reveal that while one child feels overlooked during homework time, another struggles with interrupted play. Acknowledging these feelings without judgment helps siblings feel heard and validated.

Here are key strategies for nurturing understanding and emotional support between siblings:

- Establish dedicated one-on-one time with each child daily, even if it's just 15 minutes of undivided attention
- Create safe spaces for open dialogue where siblings can express their feelings without fear of punishment or dismissal

- Develop family activities that celebrate each child's unique strengths and interests
- Teach specific ways siblings can support each other while maintaining healthy boundaries

Education plays a vital role in transforming resentment into empathy. When siblings understand that ADHD-related behaviors aren't intentional, that their brother or sister isn't choosing to be forgetful, impulsive, or emotionally reactive, it can shift their perspective dramatically. Consider creating age-appropriate explanations that help siblings understand ADHD in relatable terms.

For example, one family I worked with used the analogy of a busy traffic intersection to explain their brother's ADHD mind to his younger siblings. This simple comparison helped them understand why their brother sometimes struggled to "stop" his thoughts or actions, leading to more patience and support rather than frustration.

Implementing practical tools can also help manage sibling dynamics effectively. Here's a sample Family Meeting Agenda Template to get you started:

- Opening (5 min): Share one positive thing about each family member
- Weekly Wins (10 min): Celebrate individual and family accomplishments
- Challenges Discussion (15 min): Each person shares current struggles
- Solution Brainstorming (15 min): Family works together to address challenges

- Closing Activity (5 min): Fun family tradition or gratitude sharing

Reflection questions can help siblings process their emotions and build empathy. Consider asking:

- What's one thing you appreciate about your sibling?
- When do you feel most connected to your brother/sister?
- What would help you feel more understood in our family?
- How can we support each other better?

Remember that building empathy takes time and consistent effort. Some days will be harder than others, and that's okay. The goal isn't to eliminate all sibling conflicts; that's unrealistic in any family. Instead, focus on creating an environment where all siblings feel valued, understood, and equipped with tools to navigate challenges together.

Encourage siblings to become allies rather than adversaries by highlighting opportunities for collaboration and mutual support. This might mean having an older sibling teach a skill they're good at, or creating special sibling projects where each child's strengths contribute to shared success.

One family created what they called "Sibling Success Teams," where brothers and sisters paired up to help each other with different tasks throughout the week. The child with ADHD might help their sibling with creative projects, while the sibling could assist with organization. This approach helped build mutual appreciation for each other's strengths while providing natural opportunities for bonding.

As you work to foster understanding between siblings, maintain realistic expectations. Some days will show beautiful moments of connection and support, while others might involve more challenges. What matters most is maintaining consistency in your approach to validation, education, and open communication.

By actively addressing sibling emotions and fostering understanding, you're not just solving current family challenges; you're building stronger relationships that will last a lifetime. These early experiences in empathy and support often become the foundation for deep, meaningful sibling bonds that continue to grow stronger through the years.

Creating Fair Family Systems That Work for Everyone

"The key to family harmony isn't treating everyone exactly the same; it's ensuring everyone gets what they need to thrive." This insight from Dr. Russell Barkley captures the essence of creating fair family systems when ADHD is part of your household dynamic.[74]

Research shows that families who develop a shared understanding of ADHD and implement equitable support systems experience 27% fewer conflicts and stronger emotional connections.[74] This isn't about managing behaviors in isolation; it's about fostering an environment where every family member feels valued, understood, and supported in their unique journey.

One particularly effective approach is establishing what behavioral experts call "equity-based routines." These are daily practices that acknowledge different needs while maintaining fairness.[74] For example, morning routines might include extra transition time for your child with ADHD while giving siblings a choice in other areas of their preparation.

Here's a practical Family Meeting Agenda Template to help establish and maintain fair systems:

- Opening Circle (5 minutes): Each person shares a highlight from their week
- System Check-In (10 minutes): Review what's working/not working in current routines
- Problem-Solving (15 minutes): Address specific challenges as a team
- Role Assignment (10 minutes): Distribute weekly responsibilities based on abilities
- Celebration & Planning (5 minutes): Acknowledge successes and preview the week ahead

Reflection questions can help guide your family's journey toward more equitable systems:

- What makes each family member feel valued and supported?
- How can we adjust our routines to better meet everyone's needs?
- What strengths does each person bring to our family team?
- Where do we see opportunities for greater understanding and cooperation?

Implementing fair family systems requires several key components:

- Clear Structure with Visual Supports: Use color-coded charts or digital systems that make expectations visible for everyone[74]

- Consistent, Adapted Consequences: Implement immediate and fair responses that work for both ADHD and non-ADHD children[75, 76]

- Regular Communication Forums: Create spaces where every voice matters and concerns can be addressed openly[74]

- Individual Recognition: Celebrate each family member's unique strengths and contributions[74]

- Flexible Expectations: Adjust tasks based on each child's abilities while maintaining accountability[74]

Parental self-care plays a crucial role in maintaining these systems.[77] Studies show that parents who manage their own stress effectively are better equipped to handle family dynamics and model problem-solving skills. This might mean taking breaks when needed or seeking support from other parents facing similar challenges.

One family I worked with developed what they called their "Capability-Based Chore System." Instead of dividing tasks equally, they distributed responsibilities based on each child's strengths and challenges. Their child with ADHD excelled at active tasks like vacuuming but struggled with detailed work like folding laundry. By matching tasks to capabilities, they created a system that felt fair to everyone while setting each child up for success.

Behavioral parent training programs have shown significant success in helping families establish and maintain these systems.[75, 76] These evidence-based approaches teach parents to modify their strategies while reducing negative cycles that can affect all family members.

Remember that fair family systems evolve as your children grow and their needs change. What works today might need adjustment in six months. The key is maintaining open dialogue and a willingness to adapt while keeping core principles of fairness and support intact.

Perhaps most importantly, celebrate the small wins. When your family successfully navigates a morning routine or completes their chores without conflict, acknowledge that progress.[74] These moments of success build confidence and motivation for everyone to continue working together.

By focusing on creating systems that support everyone's needs while maintaining fairness, you're not just managing daily life; you're building a foundation for lasting family harmony and understanding.[74] Remember, the goal isn't to eliminate all challenges but to create a framework where every family member can thrive despite them.

Building Strong Sibling Bonds Through Shared Activities and Understanding

"One of the greatest gifts we can give siblings is teaching them to be advocates for each other," shared Dr. Lisa Martinez during a family workshop. "When children learn to support each other despite their differences, they build connections that last a lifetime."

Creating meaningful connections between siblings when one child has ADHD requires intentional effort and thoughtful planning. Research shows that siblings who engage in shared activities and develop mutual understanding form stronger, more resilient relationships that benefit the entire family.[71, 70, 78]

The foundation of strong sibling bonds starts with education. When siblings understand that ADHD-related behaviors aren't intentional, that their brother or sister isn't choosing to be forgetful, impulsive, or emotionally reactive, it transforms their perspective.[71, 70] This understanding creates a bridge of empathy that can last a lifetime.

Here are essential strategies for fostering positive sibling connections:

- Schedule regular "sibling time" where children engage in activities they both enjoy[71]
- Create opportunities for collaborative projects that showcase each child's strengths
- Establish shared routines that promote teamwork and mutual support[71]
- Encourage activities that naturally accommodate ADHD traits like movement and creativity[71]

One particularly effective approach is what experts call "strength-based partnering." This involves identifying activities where each sibling's unique qualities complement the other. For example, a child with ADHD might excel at generating creative ideas for a project, while their sibling helps organize and execute the plan. This collaborative approach helps both children recognize and value their differences.

The key to successful shared activities lies in their structure and selection. Choose activities that:

- Allow for natural movement and engagement[71]
- Have clear beginning and end points

- Offer opportunities for both individual and collaborative success
- Can be modified to accommodate different attention spans and energy levels

Board games, outdoor activities, and creative projects provide excellent opportunities for siblings to connect while learning to navigate challenges together.[70] These shared experiences build understanding and create positive memories that strengthen their bond.

Here's a sample Activity Planning Template to help guide shared sibling time:

- Activity Name and Goal
- Each Person's Role and Contribution
- Time Frame and Breaks Needed
- Success Markers for Both Siblings
- Celebration Plan

Reflection questions can help siblings process their shared experiences:

- What did we enjoy most about doing this together?
- How did we help each other succeed?
- What would make our next activity even better?
- What did we learn about each other today?

It's equally important to help siblings develop effective communication strategies. Teaching them to express feelings constructively, set healthy boundaries, and show appreciation for each other's efforts creates a foundation for lasting connection.[71, 70] Regular family meetings where siblings can share both challenges and victories help normalize open dialogue and mutual support.

Encourage siblings to become each other's advocates and supporters. When children with ADHD see their siblings standing up for them or celebrating their successes, it builds confidence and strengthens family bonds.[70] Similarly, when siblings without ADHD feel their efforts to understand and support are acknowledged, they're more likely to maintain that positive involvement.

Most importantly, celebrate the unique dynamic between your children. Their relationship, shaped by the presence of ADHD, often develops special qualities of patience, creativity, and resilience that can enrich their lives well into adulthood.[70, 78] By actively fostering these connections through shared activities and mutual understanding, you're helping build relationships that will support both siblings throughout their lives.

Remember that building strong sibling bonds is a journey, not a destination. There will be bumps along the way, but each challenge presents an opportunity for growth and deeper understanding. The goal isn't perfect harmony; it's creating a supportive environment where all siblings feel valued, understood, and connected.[71] "In every family's journey with ADHD, it's not the moments of perfect harmony that define us; it's how we learn to dance together through the challenges." – Patty R. Adams

As we conclude this chapter on family harmony, remember that creating a balanced and supportive environment isn't about achieving perfection; it's about fostering understanding, connection, and growth for every family member. The strategies we've explored, from implementing family meetings to developing sibling support systems, serve as building blocks for lasting family harmony.

Willa's story reminds us that when we shift our focus from managing behaviors to nurturing relationships, remarkable transformations become possible. Through their "family spotlight" system and appreciation circles, they discovered that acknowledging each family member's unique needs and contributions could transform potential points of conflict into moments of connection.

As you move forward, keep these essential principles in mind:

- Validate all emotions; both your ADHD child's and their siblings'
- Maintain clear, consistent communication about different needs and supports
- Create opportunities for individual attention and shared experiences
- Foster understanding through education and open dialogue
- Stay flexible and willing to adjust your approach as needs change
- Celebrate progress, no matter how small

Most importantly, remember that building family harmony isn't about eliminating all challenges; it's about creating an environment where every family member feels equipped to navigate those challenges together. Your family's unique dynamic, shaped by ADHD, has the potential to foster exceptional qualities of empathy, resilience, and understanding in all your children.

The reflection questions we've provided throughout this chapter can serve as ongoing tools for family discussion and growth:

- What makes each family member feel valued and supported?
- How can we better understand and respect each other's needs?
- What strengths does each person bring to our family?
- How can we support each other more effectively?

Use the Family Meeting Agenda Template as a starting point, but don't hesitate to adapt it to your family's specific needs and dynamics. Remember that consistency in communication and connection matters more than following any prescribed format perfectly.

Your family's journey with ADHD isn't just about managing symptoms; it's about growing stronger together, celebrating differences, and creating a home where everyone feels valued for exactly who they are. The challenges you face today are opportunities to build deeper understanding, stronger bonds, and lasting resilience that will benefit your family for years to come.

In the next chapter, we'll explore how to build your child's self-esteem so they can become confident and capable. But for now, take a moment to appreciate how far your family has come and the unique strengths that make your family special. Every step toward understanding, every moment of connection, and every challenge overcome together strengthens the bonds that make your family unique.

Chapter 8:

The Confidence Connection: Building Self-Esteem Through Strategic Wins

Every child deserves to feel capable and confident, yet for children with ADHD, repeated struggles with everyday tasks can chip away at their self-esteem long before they understand why things seem harder for them. As a school counselor, I've witnessed countless bright, creative students withdraw from challenges, not because they lack ability, but because years of setbacks have convinced them they can't succeed. "The size of your success is measured by the strength of your desire," leadership expert John C. Maxwell once said. These words ring especially true for children with ADHD, who often face daily challenges that can erode their sense of capability and worth.

Through my decades of counseling experience, I've seen how the cycle typically unfolds: A child struggles with tasks that seem effortless for their peers, leading to repeated disappointments that chip away at their confidence. Parents, watching their child's mounting frustration, may unknowingly compound the problem by lowering expectations or rushing to solve problems; inadvertently denying their child crucial opportunities to build resilience and experience success on their own terms.

But here's what research and experience have consistently shown: confidence isn't built through grand achievements or dramatic breakthroughs. Instead, it's cultivated through small, strategic wins that accumulate over time. It's about creating opportunities for success that are challenging enough to feel meaningful but achievable enough to build momentum.

During my third decade as a school counselor, I worked with a student named Evelyn who perfectly illustrated how strategic wins can transform a child's self-image. When we first met, Evelyn was a bright sixth-grader who would rather skip class than risk another failed assignment. Her ADHD made organizing schoolwork overwhelming, and years of incomplete projects had left her convinced she was "just stupid." Together, we created a "Success Ladder," breaking down each assignment into tiny, manageable steps. We started with just organizing her backpack, then moved to tracking one subject's homework, celebrating each small victory along the way. Within two months, Evelyn's transformation was remarkable. Not only was she completing more work, but she also began raising her hand in class and joining study groups. The pride in her voice when she said, "I actually like school now," wasn't just about better grades; it was about discovering she was capable all along. She just needed the right tools and someone to help her recognize her progress.

In this chapter, we'll explore practical strategies for building your child's confidence through intentional success experiences. You'll learn how to identify opportunities for achievement, create supportive environments that encourage positive risk-taking, and help your child recognize and celebrate their unique strengths. Most importantly, you'll discover how to shift the focus from what your child can't do to what they can; and how to build upon those capabilities systematically.

Remember, every child has inherent strengths and talents waiting to be discovered and developed. Sometimes, our most important role as parents is simply to help them uncover these gifts and provide the scaffolding they need to build confidence through experience. Let's explore how to make that happen in ways that work specifically for the ADHD brain.

Understanding the ADHD-Confidence Connection: Breaking the Cycle of Self-Doubt

"The greatest mistake we make is living in constant fear that we will make one." - John C. Maxwell's observation perfectly captures the paralyzing effect that self-doubt can have on children with ADHD. Through my years of counseling, I've watched this fear of failure grip countless bright, capable students, holding them back from reaching their true potential.

The cycle of self-doubt in children with ADHD often begins subtly but builds momentum quickly. Research shows that children with ADHD receive significantly more corrections and negative feedback than their peers, sometimes hearing thousands more critical comments before they even reach middle school.[80] This constant stream of correction doesn't just affect their daily mood; it fundamentally shapes how they view themselves and their abilities.

I witnessed this pattern with Maya, a gifted artist whose ADHD made traditional academics challenging. Each time she struggled with a math problem or forgot a homework assignment, her confidence took another hit. By the time she reached middle school, Maya had developed what psychologists call "learned helplessness," a belief that no matter what she did, she would fail.

But here's the empowering truth I've learned through decades of working with students like Maya: this cycle can be broken. The key lies in understanding that confidence isn't an innate trait; it's a skill that can be built through intentional practice and support. Just as muscles grow stronger through consistent exercise, self-confidence develops through repeated experiences of success, no matter how small.[79]

One of the most powerful ways to build confidence is through what I call "connection as the core." This approach emphasizes that a child's sense of connection to family, friends, and meaningful activities serves as a foundation for developing resilience and self-worth. Think of it as "Vitamin Connect," an essential nutrient that fuels positive growth and protects against the erosion of self-esteem.[80]

Parents play a crucial role by creating what psychologists call a "strengths-based environment." This means actively looking for and celebrating your child's unique abilities rather than focusing solely on areas that need improvement.[79] Maybe your child struggles with traditional academics but shows remarkable creativity in art or exceptional problem-solving skills in video games. These strengths aren't just hobbies; they're building blocks for confidence that can eventually transfer to other areas of life.

It's also vital to understand that children with ADHD often require more explicit support in recognizing their own progress.[81] Their challenges with executive function can make it difficult to connect today's efforts with tomorrow's results. This is where strategic praise becomes crucial, not empty compliments, but specific acknowledgment of effort, progress, and problem-solving strategies.

Breaking the cycle of self-doubt requires a shift in how we view and respond to challenges. Instead of seeing setbacks as confirmations of inadequacy, we can reframe them as opportunities for growth and learning. Take Jamie, another student I worked with, who transformed his view of making mistakes in class. Through our sessions, he learned to say, "I haven't figured this out yet" instead of "I can't do this." This simple language shift opened the door to trying new strategies instead of giving up.

Remember, the goal isn't to eliminate all struggle; that's neither possible nor desirable. Instead, we want to help our children develop the confidence to face challenges, the resilience to bounce back from setbacks, and the self-awareness to recognize their own strength and capability. When we focus on building these foundational skills, we help our children break free from the cycle of self-doubt and step into their full potential.

Strategic Success Planning: Creating Achievable Goals and Celebrating Small Wins

Think of success as building a staircase, not scaling a mountain in a single leap. For children with ADHD, this step-by-step approach isn't just helpful; it's essential. Research consistently shows that the ADHD brain responds best to clear, concrete goals with visible progress markers and immediate feedback.[83]

Let's start with what I call the "Success Ladder" template - a powerful tool I've refined over decades of counseling. Unlike traditional goal-setting approaches, the Success Ladder breaks achievements into micro-steps that work with the ADHD brain's need for quick wins and immediate reinforcement.

Here's how to build your child's Success Ladder:

- Start with the end goal at the top (Example: "Complete homework independently")
- Break it down into 5-7 concrete, observable steps
- Make each step specific and measurable
- Include a clear reward or celebration for each step
- Use visual markers to track progress

The power of this approach lies in its visibility and immediacy. For instance, with one of my students, Chris, we transformed "improve math grades" into a series of achievable daily actions: "Complete three math problems without interruption," then "Check work using the solution guide," followed by "Record completion in the progress journal."

To identify and celebrate your child's strengths, use these strategic prompts:

- "What was the best part of your day?"
- "When did you feel most proud of yourself today?"
- "What problem did you solve cleverly?"
- "What's something you did today that was hard but you kept trying?"

These questions help children recognize their own progress and build a vocabulary for their successes. Remember, celebration doesn't mean elaborate rewards; sometimes a high-five, a quick dance break, or simply naming the achievement out loud can be powerful reinforcement.

Consistency is crucial in strategic success planning. Research shows that children with ADHD benefit significantly from regular check-ins and progress reviews.[82] Establish a daily "wins review," perhaps during dinner or bedtime, where you help your child identify and celebrate their achievements, no matter how small.

One effective strategy I've seen work repeatedly is the "Success Spotlight" technique. Each evening, have your child shine a flashlight (real or metaphorical) on three things they did well that day. This simple ritual helps train the brain to notice and value progress rather than focusing solely on challenges.

Parental involvement should be strategic and gradually decreasing. Think of yourself as a scaffold that provides support while your child builds their own capability. Initially, you might help identify potential goals and break them down into steps. Over time, encourage your child to take more ownership of this process.

When setbacks occur, and they will, use them as learning opportunities rather than evidence of failure. Help your child analyze what happened and adjust their approach. Questions like "What would make this easier next time?" or "What part worked well, even if the whole thing didn't?" encourage problem-solving rather than self-criticism.

One particularly effective tool is the "Victory Journal," a simple notebook where your child records daily wins, no matter how small. The key is to make entries specific and detailed: not just "I did my homework" but "I completed my math worksheet in 20 minutes without getting distracted." This creates a growing record of success that your child can refer back to during challenging times.

Remember to match goals to your child's current capabilities while stretching them just enough to maintain interest. The sweet spot lies between too easy (which feels patronizing) and too challenging (which feels overwhelming). As one parent in my practice noted, "We started celebrating when our son remembered to put his homework in his folder. Now he's tracking all his assignments independently. Looking back, those small celebrations were actually building blocks for bigger successes."

Strategic success planning isn't just about achieving immediate goals; it's about teaching your child how to break down challenges, recognize progress, and build confidence through genuine achievement. When done consistently, this approach helps children develop not just skills, but also the self-belief that they can tackle whatever challenges come their way.

Building Resilience Through Strength-Based Parenting

"Every child is gifted," writes Dr. Lea Waters, a pioneer in positive psychology, "they just unwrap their packages at different times."[86] This profound insight captures the essence of strength-based parenting, an approach that can transform how we support children with ADHD.

Traditionally, parenting children with ADHD has often centered around fixing problems and correcting behaviors. However, research demonstrates that this deficit-focused approach can inadvertently chip away at a child's resilience and self-worth.[87] Instead, strength-based parenting flips the script by deliberately directing attention to what children do well, creating a positive feedback loop that builds both confidence and capability.[89]

The science behind this approach is compelling. Studies indicate that children with ADHD receive significantly more negative feedback than their peers throughout their day. To counter this, experts recommend maintaining at least a 5:1 ratio; that's five positive observations or comments for every corrective one.[88] This isn't about empty praise; it's about authentic recognition of your child's unique abilities and potential.

To help parents identify and nurture their child's strengths, I've developed what I call the "Strength Spotting Journal." This simple but powerful tool includes daily prompts such as:

- What did your child do today that showed persistence?
- When did you see your child's creativity shine?
- How did your child solve a problem in their own unique way?
- What positive qualities did others notice about your child today?

Think about those traits often criticized in children with ADHD: impulsivity, hyperfocus, or boundless energy. Through a strength-based lens, these same characteristics can become valuable assets. That impulsivity might actually be quick thinking in disguise. Hyperfocus, when channeled effectively, can become deep expertise in areas of interest. And that endless energy? It could be the fuel for creative problem-solving or athletic achievement.

Implementing strength-based parenting starts with careful observation. Watch for moments when your child lights up with interest or tackles challenges in unique ways. Maybe they have an exceptional memory for facts about their favorite topics, or perhaps they show remarkable empathy in social situations.[89] These are the building blocks of resilience.

One particularly powerful tool is the "strengths-to-skills" conversion model. This approach helps children reframe their natural tendencies as potential advantages.[87] For instance, if your child excels at visual thinking, encourage them to create mind maps for studying or use drawing to explain concepts to others. This not only leverages their natural abilities but also builds confidence through competence.

It's crucial to understand that strength-based parenting isn't about ignoring challenges or avoiding necessary corrections. Instead, it's about creating a foundation of confidence and capability that makes addressing difficulties more manageable. When children know their strengths, they're better equipped to tackle their challenges.[90]

The outcomes of this approach are well-documented. Research shows that children raised with strength-based parenting demonstrate higher self-esteem, reduced anxiety and depression, and improved academic performance.[86] They're more likely to develop effective coping strategies and show greater resilience in the face of setbacks.

Perhaps most importantly, strength-based parenting helps create a more positive, supportive parent-child relationship. When attention problems no longer become the defining element of your child's identity or your relationship with them, it creates space for their strengths to take center stage.

To make this approach practical, start with these daily practices:

- Begin each day by noting one strength you see in your child
- Create opportunities for your child to use their natural talents
- Share specific observations about their strengths with other family members
- Help your child identify when and how they're using their strengths

Remember, resilience isn't about never falling; it's about learning how to rise. Through strength-based parenting, we're not just managing ADHD symptoms; we're nurturing the whole child and preparing them for long-term success. When we focus on building upon what works rather than just fixing what doesn't, we help our children develop the confidence and capability they need to thrive. As we conclude this chapter on building confidence through strategic wins, let's reflect on the transformative power of intentional success experiences. We've explored how small victories, when properly structured and celebrated, can revolutionize a child's self-image and create lasting positive change.

Evelyn's journey from avoiding class to actively participating reminds us that every child has untapped potential waiting to be discovered. Her transformation wasn't just about better grades; it was about uncovering her inherent capabilities through strategic support and celebrated progress.

The key principles we've covered in this chapter include:

- The vital connection between ADHD and self-esteem, and how to break the cycle of self-doubt
- Creating and implementing Success Ladders that build confidence through achievable steps
- Using strength-based parenting to nurture resilience and capability
- The importance of maintaining a 5:1 positive-to-corrective feedback ratio

As you move forward with implementing these strategies, remember that confidence-building isn't a linear journey. There will be setbacks and challenges along the way. What matters most is maintaining consistency in your approach while adjusting strategies to match your child's unique needs and strengths.

The Success Spotting Journal, Victory Journal, and other tools we've discussed aren't just about tracking progress; they're about creating a narrative of capability that your child can carry forward. When children learn to recognize and celebrate their own progress, they develop an internal compass that guides them toward future achievements.

Perhaps most importantly, remember that your role in this process is invaluable. By maintaining a strength-based perspective and creating opportunities for strategic wins, you're not just helping your child navigate today's challenges; you're building a foundation for lifelong confidence and resilience.

As we transition to our next chapter on leveraging technology tools for ADHD success, carry forward this essential truth: every child has unique gifts and capabilities waiting to be discovered and developed. Through strategic planning, consistent support, and celebration of progress, we can help our children uncover their strengths and build the confidence they need to thrive.

Your child's journey toward confidence may not always follow a straight path, but with the strategies and insights from this chapter, you now have a roadmap for supporting their growth and celebrating their successes along the way. Remember, it's not about achieving perfection; it's about building a foundation of self-belief that will serve them well throughout their lives.

Chapter 9:

Digital Management: Technology Tools for ADHD Success

In today's digital age, technology can be either our greatest ally or our biggest distraction when managing ADHD symptoms. The key lies not in avoiding technology altogether, but in harnessing its potential to create structured, supportive systems that work with your child's ADHD brain. "In a world of endless notifications and digital distractions, the right technology can become a compass rather than a maze." - Dr. Sarah Henderson

When Annabelle first came to my office, she was struggling to keep track of her homework assignments and after-school activities. Her backpack was a jumble of crumpled papers, and her mother was at her wits' end trying to help her stay organized. During our sessions, we discovered that while traditional paper planners weren't working for Annabelle, she lit up when using digital tools. We started with a simple reminder app on her tablet, customizing it with color-coded categories and fun alert sounds. Within weeks, Annabelle was not only tracking her assignments independently but actually enjoying the process.

The transformation was remarkable; she went from missing multiple assignments per week to maintaining a digital system that kept her on track. The key wasn't just finding the right tool; it was finding one that matched her natural inclination toward technology and made organization feel less like a chore and more like a game. Six months later, Annabelle's mother tearfully shared how this digital approach had not only improved her daughter's grades but had also significantly reduced their daily stress and arguments about schoolwork.

This chapter will explore how to harness technology's potential while avoiding its pitfalls. We'll examine specific digital tools that can transform chaos into structure, resistance into engagement, and overwhelm into capability. You'll learn how to select and implement tech solutions that complement your child's ADHD brain, creating systems that stick because they work with, not against, their natural tendencies.

More importantly, we'll address the concern many parents share about screen time and digital distractions. You'll discover how to establish healthy boundaries while leveraging technology's organizational power, ensuring that digital tools serve as scaffolding for success rather than sources of scattered attention. Through practical examples and step-by-step guidance, you'll learn to identify which apps and digital strategies best match your child's needs and learning style.

As we navigate this digital landscape together, remember that technology itself is neutral; it's how we use it that matters. When thoughtfully implemented, digital tools can become powerful allies in building executive function skills, fostering independence, and creating sustainable success strategies for your child with ADHD. The goal isn't to increase screen time, but rather to make the time spent with technology more purposeful and productive.

Smart Organization: Digital Tools for Task Management and Planning

Gone are the days of single-solution planners that force ADHD brains into rigid systems. Today's digital landscape offers a rich variety of tools that can be customized to match your child's unique way of thinking and organizing information. The key is finding the right combination that makes organization feel natural rather than forced.

Let's explore some game-changing digital tools that can transform how your child manages tasks and time:

Task Management Apps

• Todoist: Perfect for visual organizers with color coding and priority flags[91]

• TickTick: Excellent for breaking down complex projects into smaller steps[92]

• Microsoft To Do: Great for simple, straightforward list-making

Calendar and Time Management

• Google Calendar: Visual time blocking with customizable reminders[94]

• TimeTimer: Digital version of the popular visual timer

• MyTime: Specifically designed for ADHD minds with dopamine-friendly rewards

Focus Enhancement Tools

• Forest: Gamifies staying on task by growing virtual trees[91]

• Focus@Will: Provides science-based music to enhance concentration

• RescueTime: Tracks digital habits and blocks distracting websites[94]

The beauty of these tools lies in their flexibility. Your child can experiment with different features until they find what resonates with their natural organizational style. For instance, if your child is visually oriented, Google Calendar's color-coding system might help them grasp time management more intuitively. If they're motivated by gaming elements, Forest's tree-growing feature could transform study sessions into engaging challenges.

When implementing digital tools, follow these essential guidelines:

- Start with one tool that addresses your child's most pressing organizational challenge
- Customize notifications and features together to ensure they're helpful, not overwhelming
- Allow time for experimentation and adjustment; finding the right system takes patience
- Celebrate small wins as your child builds confidence with their new digital supports

Remember, the goal isn't to make your child dependent on technology, but rather to use it as scaffolding while they develop their own organizational skills. As their executive function abilities grow, they can gradually take more ownership of their digital systems.

A critical aspect often overlooked is the power of cross-device synchronization.[93] When choosing tools, prioritize those that work seamlessly across devices, from school computers to home tablets. This consistency helps maintain organizational momentum regardless of where your child is working.

One parent I worked with, whose daughter struggled with assignment tracking, shared a breakthrough moment: "We tried paper planners for years, but assignments still got lost. When we switched to TickTick, my daughter could add tasks instantly from her phone, complete with photo attachments of assignment sheets. The visual reminders and progress bars spoke to her ADHD brain in a way written lists never did."

However, it's essential to maintain healthy boundaries around technology use. Work with your child to establish clear guidelines about when and how these tools should be used. For instance, you might designate specific times for checking and updating task lists, helping prevent the tools themselves from becoming a source of distraction.

Consider creating a "digital command center," a dedicated space where your child can access their organizational tools without falling into the rabbit hole of other online activities. This might include:

- A dedicated tablet or computer account for schoolwork management
- Bookmarked tabs for frequently used organizational apps
- Clear visual instructions for using each tool effectively

As your child grows more comfortable with their digital systems, you'll likely notice improved independence in other areas. The confidence gained from successfully managing tasks often translates into better self-advocacy and problem-solving skills.[94]

Remember to periodically review and adjust these systems as your child's needs evolve. What works perfectly in elementary school might need refinement in middle school or high school. The key is maintaining open communication about what's working and what needs adjustment.

Through thoughtful implementation of digital tools, we can help our children create organizational systems that don't just work; they thrive. When technology aligns with how ADHD minds naturally process information, organization transforms from a daily struggle into an achievable skill.

Focus-Enhancing Apps and Timer Technologies

"The right digital tools aren't just about managing time; they're about making time visible and manageable for the ADHD brain," counsels Dr. Thomas E. Brown, reflecting decades of research into how technology can support executive function.[95]

In today's digital landscape, timer technologies and focus-enhancing apps have revolutionized how children with ADHD can manage their attention and time. These tools serve as external brain supports, making abstract concepts like time passage concrete and visible while providing the immediate feedback that ADHD brains crave.[95, 97]

To help you navigate the vast array of available options, I've compiled a comprehensive comparison of popular focus-enhancing tools:

Visual Timer Apps
- Time Timer: Shows time passing through a disappearing colored disk
- Visual Schedule Timer: Offers customizable interval training
- Focus@Will: Combines timers with focus-enhancing music

Focus Enhancement Apps
- Forest: Grows virtual trees while staying on task
- Focus Keeper: Uses the Pomodoro technique
- Freedom: Blocks distracting apps and websites

Gamified Task Managers
- Habitica: Transforms focus into a role-playing game
- Focus Quest: Rewards sustained attention with achievements
- EpicWin: Makes task completion an adventure

When selecting focus tools for your child, look for these essential features:

- Clear visual interfaces that don't overwhelm
- Customizable notifications that work with your child's schedule
- The ability to break down time into manageable chunks
- Engaging rewards or feedback systems
- Cross-device synchronization for seamless transitions

A school counselor I worked with shared a powerful success story about Daniel, who struggled with getting lost in tasks, often spending three hours on a 30-minute assignment. By introducing the Time Timer app, Marcus could finally 'see' time passing, which helped him pace his work and stay on track. Within weeks, he was completing assignments within reasonable timeframes and feeling more confident about his ability to manage his time.

However, it's essential to remember that technology should serve as a support tool, not a crutch.[95, 98] Start with one app or timer that addresses your child's most pressing focus challenge. Once they've mastered that tool, you can gradually introduce others as needed. This prevents overwhelm and builds confidence through successful adoption.

To maximize the effectiveness of these tools, consider implementing these practical strategies:

- Set up the tool together, making it visually appealing and intuitive for your child
- Start with short focus periods and gradually increase duration as success builds
- Use the tools consistently across different environments (home, homework space, etc.)
- Celebrate progress and adjust settings as your child's needs evolve

Parental controls and screen time management are crucial considerations when implementing digital focus tools.[95, 97] Many apps now include built-in limits and monitoring features to help maintain healthy boundaries. For instance, Forest allows parents to set daily usage limits while still maintaining the app's engaging tree-growing feature.

One common concern I hear from parents is whether using technology to build focus might create dependency. Research suggests that when implemented thoughtfully, these tools actually help children develop better internal time awareness and self-regulation skills.[95, 96] Think of them as training wheels; temporary supports that help build lasting capabilities.

The beauty of modern focus-enhancing tools lies in their ability to grow with your child.[95, 96] As their needs evolve, these systems can be adjusted to support increasing independence and complexity in their academic and personal lives. The key is finding the right combination of tools that makes time management feel less like a burden and more like a natural extension of how their mind works.

By thoughtfully implementing these digital supports, you're not just helping your child manage their time and attention today; you're helping them develop crucial skills that will serve them well into the future.[95, 97, 98] Remember, the goal isn't perfection; it's progress. Celebrate the small wins as your child develops these essential skills, and be patient with the learning curve.

One mother shared how her daughter went from dreading study sessions to actually looking forward to them after they started using the Forest app: "Watching her virtual garden grow while she completes her work has transformed homework time from a battle into something she genuinely enjoys. The visual reward of a flourishing forest has made focusing tangible and achievable."

As you explore these tools with your child, remember that finding the right fit might take some trial and error. What works brilliantly for one child might not resonate with another. The key is to approach the process with patience and flexibility, allowing your child to help guide the selection of tools that feel most natural and effective for their unique way of thinking.

Creating Healthy Digital Boundaries and Screen Time Balance

"The key to digital wellness isn't about restriction; it's about creating intentional spaces where technology serves your child's growth rather than hijacks their attention," notes Dr. Rachel Martinez, highlighting a crucial shift in how we approach screen time management for children with ADHD.[102]

In today's hyper-connected world, children with ADHD face unique challenges when it comes to managing screen time and digital boundaries. Their natural tendency toward hyperfocus combined with the dopamine-rich environment of digital media can create a perfect storm for excessive screen use. But here's the truth: it's not about eliminating technology; it's about creating a structure that works with your child's ADHD brain.

Let's explore effective strategies for creating healthy digital boundaries that actually work for ADHD minds:

- Create designated tech-free zones and times, especially in bedrooms and during meals[101]
- Break screen time into shorter, more manageable chunks rather than long stretches[99]
- Use parental control apps strategically to automate limits and reduce power struggles[99,100]
- Keep devices in common areas where usage can be naturally monitored[101]
- Establish clear before-bed routines that transition away from screens[101, 102]

One family I worked with transformed their daily battles over screen time by implementing what they called the "Tech Triangle," clear boundaries around when, where, and how long devices could be used. Their 12-year-old son, who previously fought every limit, actually began self-regulating his screen time once he understood the structure and participated in setting the rules.

To support effective implementation, consider this practical framework:

- Daily schedules with clear, consistent device use times[99]
- Physical activity paired with screen time to create natural transitions[99]
- Visual timers make limits concrete and understandable[99, 101, 102]
- Automated cut-offs to reduce negotiations[99]
- Designated charging stations outside bedrooms[100]

Remember, the goal isn't perfect compliance; it's progress toward healthy habits. When children understand the 'why' behind digital boundaries and feel ownership in the process, they're more likely to develop lasting self-regulation skills.

One effective approach involves using natural stopping points in games or activities rather than arbitrary time limits.[102] This works better with the ADHD brain's need for closure and completion. Consider incorporating physically engaging screens like active gaming systems that combine movement with digital play.[100]

I worked with a family who discovered that their daughter managed screen time better when they used a visual schedule showing both screen and non-screen activities. The predictability reduced anxiety about when she would next have access to her devices, making transitions smoother and reducing emotional meltdowns.

Another crucial aspect is modeling healthy digital habits. Children learn more from what we do than what we say. Consider establishing family-wide digital boundaries that everyone follows, such as device-free dinner times or morning routines without screens. This creates a culture of intentional technology use rather than constant connectivity.

When implementing digital boundaries, consistency is key, but flexibility within structure is essential. Some days might require more structure than others, and that's okay. The important thing is maintaining a framework that supports your child's development while managing screen time effectively.

For older children and teens, involve them in creating their own digital wellness plan. This might include:

- Setting personal goals for balanced technology use
- Identifying potential triggers for excessive screen time
- Creating strategies for managing online distractions
- Developing alternative activities for entertainment and relaxation

Remember to celebrate progress rather than perfection. When your child successfully follows digital boundaries or shows improved self-regulation, acknowledge these wins. This positive reinforcement helps build confidence in their ability to manage their digital world.

Most importantly, maintain perspective. Every family's approach to digital boundaries will look different. What matters is finding a balance that works for your child and your family's needs while supporting healthy development and ADHD management. With clear structure, consistent implementation, and collaborative planning, you can help your child develop a healthy relationship with technology that supports rather than hinders their success. As we conclude our exploration of digital tools and ADHD management, remember that technology isn't inherently good or bad; it's how we harness its power that makes the difference. Throughout this chapter, we've discovered how thoughtfully selected digital tools can transform chaos into structure, resistance into engagement, and overwhelm into capability.

The journey to finding the right digital support system isn't about implementing every new app or tool available. It's about understanding your child's unique needs and carefully selecting solutions that complement their natural tendencies while building essential skills. Whether it's using visual timers to make time tangible, task management apps to create clear pathways for success, or focus-enhancement tools to build concentration muscles, the key lies in matching the tool to your child's specific challenges and strengths.

Annabelle's story reminds us that technology, when thoughtfully implemented, can become a powerful ally in developing executive function skills and fostering independence. Her transformation from struggling with basic organization to confidently managing her academic responsibilities demonstrates the profound impact of finding the right digital supports.

As you move forward, keep these essential principles in mind:

- Start small and build gradually, allowing mastery of one tool before introducing another
- Focus on solutions that enhance your child's natural abilities rather than forcing them into rigid systems

- Maintain healthy boundaries around screen time while leveraging technology's organizational power
- Celebrate progress and adjust strategies as your child's needs evolve

The digital landscape will continue to evolve, bringing new tools and possibilities for supporting children with ADHD. By establishing strong foundations now, understanding how to select, implement, and balance digital supports, you're equipping your child with skills that will serve them well into the future.

Most importantly, remember that the goal isn't perfection. It's about progress, about finding those small wins that build confidence and competence over time. Every step forward, no matter how small, is a victory worth celebrating. As you continue this journey, trust that with the right tools and support, your child can develop systems that not only help them manage their ADHD but also allow their unique gifts to shine.

You're not just teaching them to use technology; you're showing them how to become capable, confident individuals who can harness the power of digital tools to support their success. And that's a gift that will keep giving long after the apps are closed and the devices are put away.

Chapter 10:

Future Forward: Preparing Your ADHD Child for Long-Term Independence

The journey toward independence for a child with ADHD isn't marked by a single milestone, but rather by thousands of small steps forward. As we prepare our children for their future, we must carefully balance protective instincts with the essential need to let them develop their own problem-solving muscles. Sometimes the smallest step in the right direction ends up being the biggest step of your life, as Emma Seppala wisely noted. This truth becomes especially poignant as we guide our children with ADHD toward independence. The path isn't always straight or predictable, but each small victory builds the foundation for lasting success. As parents, we often grapple with a delicate balance: wanting to protect our children while recognizing that true growth comes from allowing them to navigate challenges with gradually decreasing support.

During a parent consultation session, Blake, a sixteen-year-old with ADHD, surprised me with his innovative solution to managing his college application process. Instead of relying on his parents' constant reminders, he had created a personalized system using his smartphone, complete with customized alarms, visual checklists, and reward milestones. When his mother expressed concern about him handling the process independently, Blake confidently demonstrated how he'd broken down each task into manageable chunks and set up accountability checks with his mentor. This moment perfectly illustrated how, with the right support and tools, our ADHD children can develop their own strategies for independence. Blake's mother later shared that stepping back, though terrifying, allowed her son to discover his capabilities and build genuine confidence in his ability to navigate complex responsibilities.

This chapter marks a crucial transition in our journey together. We've explored various strategies for supporting your child's academic success, emotional regulation, and organizational skills. Now, we'll focus on how to gradually transfer these tools and responsibilities to your child's capable hands. The goal isn't perfect independence; even neurotypical adults rely on support systems and tools. Instead, we're aiming for confident capability: the ability to recognize when help is needed and how to seek it effectively.

As we delve into practical strategies for building lasting independence, remember that this isn't about pushing your child toward premature self-sufficiency. It's about carefully scaffolding their growth, celebrating their unique problem-solving approaches, and helping them develop the self-advocacy skills they'll need for adult life. Whether they're heading to college, entering the workforce, or charting their own unique path, the tools and confidence they develop now will serve as their foundation for future success.

Building Self-Advocacy Skills: Teaching Your Child to Speak Up and Seek Support

Teaching your child to advocate for themselves is one of the most valuable gifts you can offer; it's the key that unlocks doors to lifelong success. But what exactly does effective self-advocacy look like for a child with ADHD? At its core, it's about developing three essential skills: self-awareness, clear communication, and problem-solving abilities.

Let's start with a practical framework I call the "SPEAK UP" method:

- Self-awareness: Understanding their unique needs and challenges
- Plan: Preparing what to say and how to say it
- Express: Communicating needs clearly and respectfully
- Advocate: Asking for specific support or accommodations
- Know rights: Understanding what help they're entitled to
- Use resources: Identifying and accessing available support
- Practice: Regular rehearsal of advocacy skills

Begin by helping your child develop deeper self-awareness about their ADHD profile. Instead of broad statements like "I can't focus," guide them to identify specific situations: "I concentrate better when I use my noise-canceling headphones during tests" or "I remember instructions more easily when they're written down." This precise understanding becomes the foundation for effective advocacy.

Create what I call an "advocacy toolkit," a personalized collection of phrases, strategies, and approaches that work for your child. For example, teach them to say: "Could you please explain that in a different way?" or "I understand better when I can see the instructions written down." These aren't rigid scripts but flexible tools they can adapt to different situations.

One effective strategy is the "Practice-Reflect-Adjust" cycle. Start with low-stakes situations at home, like asking for help with a household task, before moving to more challenging scenarios like discussing accommodations with teachers. After each advocacy attempt, guide your child through reflection questions: What worked well? What could they try differently next time? This builds both confidence and competence.

Remember that timing and approach matter significantly. I often teach students the "green zone" concept; identifying when they're calm and focused as the best times to advocate for themselves. This might mean speaking to a teacher before class starts rather than during a lesson, or requesting a meeting to discuss accommodations rather than bringing up concerns in the middle of an assignment.

Encourage what I call "solution-focused advocacy." Rather than simply stating problems, guide your child to present potential solutions. For instance, instead of saying "I can't finish my work in class," they might say "Would it be possible for me to have extra time to complete assignments?" This approach demonstrates responsibility and problem-solving skills.

Create opportunities for your child to practice self-advocacy in real-world situations. Start small; perhaps having them order their own meal at a restaurant or ask a librarian for help finding a book. As their confidence grows, they can tackle more significant advocacy challenges, like explaining their learning needs to a new teacher or coach.

Just as importantly, help your child understand that seeking support is a sign of strength, not weakness. Share examples of successful adults who actively advocate for their needs. You might say, "You know, even Olympic athletes have coaches and support teams; asking for help is part of being successful."

Document what works in what I call a "success file," a collection of effective advocacy strategies and positive outcomes. This becomes a powerful resource your child can refer to when facing new challenges. It might include specific accommodations that have helped in the past, phrases that worked well with teachers, or techniques for managing overwhelming situations.

Remember that building self-advocacy skills is a gradual process. There will be successes and setbacks along the way. Celebrate the efforts, not just the outcomes. Each time your child speaks up for themselves, they're strengthening their advocacy muscles and moving closer to independent success.

As one parent in my practice beautifully expressed, "Teaching my daughter to advocate for herself was like watching her find her voice; not just any voice, but her own powerful, confident voice." That's really what self-advocacy is about: empowering our children to speak up, seek support, and take charge of their own success story.

Financial Literacy and Executive Function: Managing Money with an ADHD Brain

Understanding money shouldn't feel like solving a complex puzzle, yet for many individuals with ADHD, financial management presents unique challenges that go far beyond simple budgeting. The executive function differences that affect planning, impulse control, and time perception can make handling money feel overwhelming, but with the right strategies, your child can develop strong financial skills that work with their natural thinking patterns.

Let's start with a practical framework I call the "Money Mastery Blueprint," a step-by-step approach to building financial literacy skills that accommodates ADHD thinking patterns:

- Make it Visual: Create concrete, visible systems for tracking money
- Master the Basics: Focus on fundamental skills before complex concepts
- Break it Down: Divide financial tasks into smaller, manageable steps
- Automate Success: Use technology to bypass executive function challenges
- Review and Adjust: Regular check-ins to celebrate progress and refine strategies

The key to teaching financial literacy to ADHD brains lies in making abstract concepts tangible and immediate. Traditional advice about saving for the future often falls flat because the ADHD brain lives primarily in the present moment. Instead of lecturing about long-term savings, create a visual money system where your child can physically see their progress.

Consider Tammy, a teenager I worked with who struggled with impulsive spending. We created a "Smart Spending Station" in her room; three clear jars labeled "Now," "Soon," and "Later." Each time she received money, she would physically divide it among the jars, making the abstract concept of budgeting concrete and visible. This simple system helped her develop awareness of spending choices and experience the satisfaction of watching her savings grow.

Automation becomes your best friend in managing the executive function challenges that impact money management. Help your child set up automatic transfers for savings, use apps that track spending in real-time, and establish regular financial check-ins. Think of it as creating external structures to support internal growth.

Break down financial goals into SMART objectives (Specific, Measurable, Achievable, Relevant, Time-bound). Instead of a vague goal like "save money," work with your child to set specific targets: "Save $20 each week for the next month toward that new gaming console." This approach provides clear benchmarks and immediate feedback, essential for the ADHD brain.

Teaching delayed gratification requires a different approach for ADHD minds. Create what I call "success stepping stones," smaller, more immediate rewards while building toward bigger financial goals. For example, when your child successfully follows their budget for a week, they might earn a small privilege while still progressing toward their larger saving goal.

Regular financial check-ins are crucial, but keep them short and positive. I recommend the "5-5-5 Review": 5 minutes to celebrate successes, 5 minutes to identify challenges, and 5 minutes to adjust strategies. This structured approach prevents overwhelm while maintaining accountability.

Address impulse spending head-on by creating a "Pause and Plan" protocol. Teach your child to implement a 24-hour rule for unplanned purchases over a certain amount. During this time, they can research the item, consider alternatives, and evaluate whether it aligns with their financial goals.

Don't forget to harness your child's ADHD strengths in their financial journey. Many individuals with ADHD excel at finding creative solutions and thinking outside the box. Encourage these talents by involving them in family budget discussions or brainstorming ways to earn money through their unique interests and abilities.

Remember that setbacks are learning opportunities, not failures. When impulse purchases or planning challenges occur, use them as chances to refine strategies and build problem-solving skills. The goal isn't perfect financial management; it's developing a sustainable approach that works with your child's unique brain wiring.

Finally, consider creating a "Financial Independence Roadmap" that outlines progressive money management responsibilities as your child matures. Start with basic concepts like tracking spending and gradually introduce more complex skills like maintaining a checking account or using a debit card. This structured progression builds confidence while ensuring your child develops essential financial capabilities for adult life.

With patience, the right tools, and consistent support, children with ADHD can develop strong financial literacy skills that serve them well into adulthood. The key lies in working with their natural thinking patterns while building external systems that support success.

Transitioning to Adult Life: Creating Scaffolded Independence

The road to independence isn't a straight line; it's a series of carefully planned steps, each building upon the last. Research shows that young adults with ADHD are eleven times more likely than their peers to face challenges in employment and education[115]. However, this statistic isn't destiny; it's a call to action for thoughtful transition planning.

Think of scaffolded independence like teaching someone to ride a bike. You begin with training wheels, offering complete support. Gradually, you raise those training wheels, allowing for small wobbles while maintaining safety. Eventually, you run alongside, providing reassurance without direct support. Finally, you watch proudly as they pedal away on their own, knowing you're still there if needed.

A successful transition requires strategic planning in several key areas:

- Life Skills Development: Daily living tasks, personal care, and home management
- Financial Management: Budgeting, banking, and responsible spending
- Healthcare Navigation: Managing medications, appointments, and self-advocacy
- Educational/Vocational Planning: College preparation or career path development
- Social Support Networks: Building and maintaining relationships

Start by implementing what I call the "Independence Inventory," a comprehensive assessment of your child's current capabilities and areas for growth. Rather than focusing on deficits, identify strengths that can serve as building blocks for new skills. For instance, if your teen excels at using technology, leverage this strength by introducing apps for medication management or calendar organization.

One crucial aspect often overlooked is the maintenance of support systems during transition periods. Research indicates that many young adults with ADHD disengage from treatment services during this crucial time,[114] often due to stigma or changes in their support network. Create a clear plan for transitioning from pediatric to adult healthcare services, ensuring continuous access to necessary medical and mental health support.

Vocational preparation becomes increasingly important during this phase. Early exposure to work environments through part-time jobs, internships, or volunteer positions provides invaluable real-world experience. These opportunities aren't just about building a resume; they're controlled testing grounds where mistakes become learning opportunities rather than career setbacks.

Teach what I call "strategic self-advocacy," the ability to recognize when help is needed and how to seek it effectively. This might include role-playing common workplace scenarios or practicing how to discuss accommodations with professors. Remember, independence doesn't mean doing everything alone; it means knowing how to access and utilize available support systems.

The transition to financial independence requires particular attention for individuals with ADHD. Create a graduated system of financial responsibility, starting with basic budgeting and progressing to more complex financial management. Use visual tools and automated systems to support executive function challenges while building money management skills.

Implement what I call the "Gradual Release Protocol," a systematic approach to transferring responsibility:

- Observation Phase: Your child watches as you model the task
- Collaborative Phase: You work together, sharing responsibility
- Guided Independence: They take the lead while you supervise
- Full Independence: They manage the task independently

Document successes and challenges in a "Transition Journal." This record helps track progress while identifying areas that might need additional support or modified strategies. It also serves as a confidence boost, showing your child how far they've come.

Remember that setbacks are normal and even necessary parts of the learning process. When challenges arise, resist the urge to step in immediately. Instead, guide your child through problem-solving steps: What happened? What options exist? What could work better next time?

As one parent in my practice wisely noted, "We're not just preparing our kids for independence; we're preparing ourselves to step back and trust in their capabilities." This journey requires patience, flexibility, and faith in your child's ability to grow into their own unique version of independence.

Most importantly, celebrate progress along the way. Each small step, whether it's remembering to refill a prescription, successfully managing a work schedule, or navigating public transportation, represents growth toward independent living. These victories, however small they might seem, are essential building blocks for long-term success.

The goal isn't perfect independence; even neurotypical adults rely on support systems and tools. Instead, aim for what I call "capable independence," the ability to manage daily life while recognizing when and how to seek help when needed. With thoughtful planning, consistent support, and gradual stepping back, you can help your child develop the skills and confidence needed for a fulfilling adult life. As we conclude this chapter and our journey together, I'm reminded of Blake's innovative approach to managing his college applications. His story exemplifies what becomes possible when we equip our children with the right tools while having the courage to step back and let them lead. It's a powerful reminder that independence isn't about perfect execution; it's about developing the confidence and capability to navigate life's challenges effectively.

Through our exploration of self-advocacy, financial literacy, and transition planning, we've uncovered essential truths about preparing ADHD children for adulthood. We've learned that independence doesn't mean doing everything alone; it means knowing when and how to seek help. We've discovered that financial management isn't about perfect budgeting; it's about creating systems that work with your child's unique brain wiring. And we've seen that the path to independence isn't a straight line but rather a gradual journey of growing capability and confidence.

The strategies we've explored, from the "SPEAK UP" method for self-advocacy to the "Money Mastery Blueprint" for financial literacy, aren't just techniques. They're building blocks for a foundation of lasting independence. Each tool, whether it's creating visual systems for money management or practicing strategic self-advocacy, is designed to work with your child's ADHD brain rather than against it.

As you move forward with your child's transition to independence, remember that progress isn't always linear, and setbacks are natural parts of the journey. What matters most is maintaining a supportive environment that encourages growth while providing the structure needed for success. Trust in the "Gradual Release Protocol" we discussed; observe, collaborate, guide, and then step back as your child demonstrates readiness for each new level of independence.

Your role in this journey is evolving from primary manager to supportive guide. This transition might feel challenging at times, but remember, you're not just preparing your child for independence. You're helping them discover their own capacity for resilience, innovation, and success. The confidence they build through each small victory, whether it's successfully managing their first bank account or advocating for accommodations in a new situation, creates momentum for future achievements.

As we close this chapter, I want to leave you with this thought: Your child's path to independence may look different from what you initially imagined, and that's okay. Success isn't measured by how closely they follow traditional paths but by how effectively they learn to navigate their own journey. With your guidance, understanding, and the strategies we've explored together, they have everything they need to build a future that celebrates their unique strengths and embraces their challenges as opportunities for growth.

Remember, you're walking alongside your child on this journey, gradually adjusting your support as they develop their capabilities. Trust in their ability to grow, believe in their potential to thrive, and keep celebrating every step forward on their path to independence. The future is bright for your child; not despite their ADHD, but because they've learned to harness its unique strengths while developing tools to manage its challenges effectively.

Conclusion

As we draw our journey to a close, I'm reminded of a truth that has anchored my four decades in education: every child with ADHD possesses extraordinary potential waiting to be unlocked. The key isn't found in trying to 'fix' them or force them into traditional molds; it lies in understanding their unique neural wiring and creating environments where their natural strengths can flourish.

Through these pages, we've explored the intricate relationship between dopamine and motivation, discovered the power of brain-friendly organization systems, and witnessed how strategic wins build lasting confidence. We've learned that success isn't about pushing harder; it's about working smarter, with tools and approaches specifically designed for the ADHD mind.

Remember Aurora from our opening chapter? Her transformation from an overwhelmed student to a confident learner embodies the heart of our message: when we understand and work with our children's unique operating systems, rather than against them, remarkable growth becomes possible. The strategies we've explored, from creating dopamine-friendly study environments to implementing visual organization systems, aren't just techniques; they're pathways to independence, self-worth, and academic achievement.

As you continue your parenting journey, remember that progress rarely follows a straight line. There will be challenges and setbacks, but these aren't failures; they're opportunities to adjust and refine your approach. Every small victory, every moment of increased independence, and every instance where your child feels capable and understood is a step in the right direction.

You aren't alone on this path. The insights and strategies shared here come from decades of experience working with families just like yours. They've been tested, refined, and proven effective in real-world situations. Your commitment to understanding and supporting your child's unique needs is already making a profound difference.

Perhaps most importantly, carry with you the knowledge that your child's ADHD isn't a limitation; it's simply a different way of perceiving and interacting with the world. With understanding, appropriate support, and the right tools, your child can not only manage their ADHD but harness its unique attributes to achieve remarkable things.

Your role in this journey isn't about reaching a final destination; it's about continuous growth, adaptation, and celebration of progress. Trust in the process, believe in your child's potential, and keep building those bridges to success, one strategic step at a time. The tools and understanding you've gained here will serve as your compass, helping you navigate challenges and celebrate victories along the way.

Today's small wins lay the foundation for tomorrow's achievements. You have the knowledge, the strategies, and the strength to guide your child toward a future filled with confidence, capability, and success. The journey continues, and the brightest chapters are still to come.

References

[1] Burger, T. (2023, December 22). *The Link Between ADHD and Executive Function Deficits*. Student Evaluation Center. https://www.studentevalcenter.com/blog-2-1/the-link-between-adhd-and-executive-function-deficits

[2] Henley, M. (2024, October 15). *The Role of Executive Function in ADHD*. Animo Sano Psychiatry. https://animosanopsychiatry.com/the-role-of-executive-function-in-adhd/

[3] Barkley, R. (2019, October 3). *What Is Executive Function? 7 Deficits Tied to ADHD*. ADDitude Magazine. https://www.additudemag.com/7-executive-function-deficits-linked-to-adhd/

[4] The Team at Well Roots Counseling. (2023, September 7). *Executive Functioning: Boost Your Brain's Command Center*. Well Roots Counseling. https://www.wellrootscounseling.com/blog/executive-functioning-boost-your-brains-command-center

[5] Wilkins, F. (2024, April 10). *How Is the ADHD Brain Different?*. Child Mind Institute. https://childmind.org/article/how-is-the-adhd-brain-different/

[6] Volkow N. D. (2009, September 9). *Evaluating Dopamine Reward Pathway in ADHD: Clinical Implications*. JAMA. https://pmc.ncbi.nlm.nih.gov/articles/PMC2958516/

[7] Rosch K. S. (2013, August 29). *The effects of performance-based rewards on neurophysiological correlates of stimulus, error, and*

feedback processing in children with ADHD. PMC - US National Library of Medicine. https://pmc.ncbi.nlm.nih.gov/articles/PMC3807761/

[8] Embracing You Therapy. (2023, March 13). *How the Reward System in ADHD Affects Motivation.* Embracing You Therapy. https://embracingyoutherapy.com/how-the-reward-system-in-adhd-affects-motivation/

[9] Benisek, A. (2024, June 14). *ADHD and Dopamine: What's the Connection?.* WebMD. https://www.webmd.com/add-adhd/childhood-adhd/adhd-dopamine

[10] Brennan A. R., Arnsten A. F. T. (2008). *Neuronal Mechanisms Underlying Attention Deficit Hyperactivity Disorder: The Influence of Arousal on Prefrontal Cortical Function.* Annals of the New York Academy of Sciences. https://pmc.ncbi.nlm.nih.gov/articles/PMC2863119/

[11] Rubia K. (2018, March 28). *Cognitive Neuroscience of Attention Deficit Hyperactivity Disorder (ADHD) and Its Clinical Translation.* Frontiers in Human Neuroscience. https://www.frontiersin.org/journals/human-neuroscience/articles/10.3389/fnhum.2018.00100/full

[12] Arnsten AFT. (2009, May 1). *The Emerging Neurobiology of Attention Deficit Hyperactivity Disorder: The Key Role of the Prefrontal Association Cortex.* Journal of Pediatrics. https://pmc.ncbi.nlm.nih.gov/articles/PMC2894421/

[13] Silver, L. M. (2025, July 28). *The Neuroscience of the ADHD Brain.* ADDitude Magazine. https://www.additudemag.com/neuroscience-of-adhd-brain/

[14] Littman, E. (2025, July 28). *Never Enough? Why ADHD Brains Crave Stimulation.* ADDitude Magazine. https://www.additudemag.com/brain-stimulation-and-adhd-cravings-dependency-and-regulation/

[15] BetterHelp Editorial Team. (2025, July 28). *The Link Between Dopamine And ADHD: How Does It Work?.* BetterHelp. https://www.betterhelp.com/advice/adhd/the-link-between-dopamine-and-adhd/

[16] The Childhood Collective. (2021, October 13). *10 Do's and Don'ts for Using Rewards to Improve Your Child's Challenging Behavior.* The Childhood Collective. https://thechildhoodcollective.com/2021/10/13/10-dos-and-donts-for-using-rewards-to-improve-your-childs-challenging-behavior/

[17] (n.d.) https://ccf.fiu.edu/research/assets/howtoestablishaschooldrc.pdf

[18] Evoke Learning. (2024, December 10). *School-Home Daily Report Cards for Students with ADHD.* Evoke Learning. https://www.evokelearning.ca/blog/school-home-daily-report-cards-for-students-with-adhd/

[19] (n.d.) https://www.cincinnatichildrens.org/-/media/Cincinnati-Childrens/Home/patients/family-support-resources/behavioral-

management/page-media/Contingency-Management-Systems-for-Children-with-ADHD.pdf

[20] Diary of an ADHD Strategist. (2025, March 30). *The Power of Small Wins for ADHD: Recognizing Growth on Your Journey*. Diary of an ADHD Strategist https://elidervonte.substack.com/p/the-power-of-small-wins-for-adhd

[21] Menon, Dr. (2025, March 10). *ADHD and Motivation: How to Start Tasks and Stay on Track*. My Thrive Collective. https://mythrivecollective.com/adhd-and-motivation-how-to-start-tasks-and-stay-on-track/

[22] Abbey Neuropsychology Clinic. (2024, December). *ADHD and Self-Esteem: Boosting Confidence in Your Child*. Abbey Neuropsychology Clinic. https://www.abbeyneuropsychologyclinic.com/adhd-and-self-esteem-boosting-confidence-in-your-child/

[23] Kids Empowered 4 Life. (2023, January 24). *Motivation & ADHD*. Kids Empowered 4 Life. https://kidsempowered4life.com/motivation-adhd/

[24] Minnesota Neuropsychology. (2024, March 29). *Inertia to Momentum in ADHD*. Minnesota Neuropsychology. https://www.mnneuropsychology.com/articles/inertia-to-momentum.html

[25] Carames C. N., Irwin L. N., & Kofler M. J. (2021, September 8). *Is There a Relation Between Visual-Motor Integration and Academic Achievement in School-Aged Children with and without ADHD?*.

PMC - US National Library of Medicine National Institutes of Health. https://pmc.ncbi.nlm.nih.gov/articles/PMC8727494/

[26] Effective Students. (2024, October). *Classroom Strategies for Teaching Students with ADHD*. Effective Students. https://effectivestudents.com/articles/classroom-strategies-for-teaching-students-with-adhd/

[27] Thomas N., Karuppali S. (2022, January 1). *The Efficacy of Visual Activity Schedule Intervention in Reducing Problem Behaviors in Children With Attention-Deficit/Hyperactivity Disorder Between the Ages of 5 and 12 Years: A Systematic Review*. Journal of the Korean Academy of Child and Adolescent Psychiatry. https://pmc.ncbi.nlm.nih.gov/articles/PMC8733412/

[28] Behaviour Help. (2023, December 15). *Empowering Learners: Differentiating the curriculum for students with ADHD*. Behaviour Help. https://behaviourhelp.com/behaviour-blog/positive-behaviour-support/empowering-learners-differentiating-the-curriculum-for-students-with-adhd

[29] Hitomi, M. (2022, August 31). *ADHD friendly organization strategies for back to school*. Tiimo. https://www.tiimoapp.com/resource-hub/adhd-friendly-organization-strategies-for-back-to-school

[30] PrivateADHD. (2025, July 29). *How to Study with ADHD: 14 Effective Strategies for Academic Success*. PrivateADHD. https://www.privateadhd.com/blog/how-to-study-with-adhd-14-effective-strategies-for-academic-success

[31] ADDA Editorial Team. (2023, August 30). *How to Study Efficiently with ADHD: 7 Tips to Boost Focus & Motivation*. ADDA - Attention Deficit Disorder Association. https://add.org/tips-for-studying-with-adhd/

[32] Henshaw, A. (2024, January 17). *ADHD-Friendly Study Habits for Students: A Fresh Approach for the New Semester*. Done First. https://www.donefirst.com/blog/adhd-friendly-study-habits-for-students-a-fresh-approach-for-the-new-semester

[33] Faculty of Health and Behavioural Sciences. (2022, November 14). *5 secrets to studying better with ADHD*. Faculty of Health and Behavioural Sciences, The University of Queensland. https://habs.uq.edu.au/blog/2022/11/5-secrets-studying-better-adhd

[34] Lynn, T. (2025, May). *ADHD Command Center: Organize Your Life Today*. Declutter in Minutes. https://declutterinminutes.com/adhd-command-center/

[35] Bryan, Beth. (2024, August). *Get Organized with an ADHD Friendly Family Command Center*. Beth Bryan. https://bethbryan.com/2024/08/get-organized-with-an-adhd-friendly-family-command-center/

[36] Lemon Lime Adventures. (2014, September). *Organizing Life with a Family Command Center*. Lemon Lime Adventures. https://lemonlimeadventures.com/organize-life-family-command-center/

[37] ADDA Editorial Team. (2024, January 29). *ADHD Emotional Dysregulation: Managing Intense Emotions*. ADDA - Attention

Deficit Disorder Association. https://add.org/emotional-dysregulation-adhd/

[38] Kravit, A. (2025, May 09). *Everything You Never Knew About the ADHD Brain*. ADDitude Magazine. https://www.additudemag.com/adhd-brain-prefrontal-cortex-attention-emotions/

[39] Hassall, J. (2020, October). *Adult ADHD and Emotions*. CHADD. https://chadd.org/attention-article/adult-adhd-and-emotions/

[40] Ojha A., Jones N. P., Teague H., Versace A., Gnagy E. M., Joseph H. M., Molina B. S. G., Ladouceur C. D. (2024, February). *Biological Psychiatry: Cognitive Neuroscience Neuroimaging - Altered Lateral Prefrontal Cortex Functioning During Emotional Interference Resistance Is Associated with Affect Lability in Adults with Persisting Symptoms of ADHD from Childhood*. University of Pittsburgh Department of Psychiatry. https://www.psychiatry.pitt.edu/biological-psychiatry-cognitive-neuroscience-neuroimaging-altered-lateral-prefrontal-cortex

[41] Connaughton M. (2023, November 2). *The Limbic System in Children and Adolescents With Attention-Deficit/Hyperactivity Disorder: A Longitudinal Structural Magnetic Resonance Imaging Analysis*. Biological Psychiatry Global Open Science. https://pmc.ncbi.nlm.nih.gov/articles/PMC10829648/

[42] Williams, C. (2022, November 14). *Self-Regulation for Children with ADHD*. Summit Education. https://summit-education.com/blog/general/self-regulation-for-children-with-adhd/

[43] Williams, P. (2023, December). *Behavior Strategies for Raising Kids with ADHD*. CHADD. https://chadd.org/adhd-news/adhd-news-caregivers/attention-behavior-strategies-for-raising-kids-with-adhd/

[44] Rouse M. H. (2025, June 20). *How Can We Help Kids With Self-Regulation?*. Child Mind Institute. https://childmind.org/article/can-help-kids-self-regulation/

[45] Buzanko, C. (2025, June 18). *The Key to ADHD Emotional Regulation? Cultivating Gratitude, Pride & Compassion*. ADDitude Magazine. https://www.additudemag.com/emotional-regulation-adhd-kids-strategies/

[46] Spencer, N. (2022, July 15). *How to Create a Productive Study Environment for Students with ADHD and Other Special Needs*. rtor.org. https://www.rtor.org/2022/07/15/how-to-create-a-productive-study-environment-for-students-with-adhd/

[47] Rudinski, A. (2023, May 2). *What Environment Is Best For People With ADHD To Learn?*. The Ladder Method. https://www.theladdermethod.com/blog/what-environment-is-best-for-people-with-adhd-to-learn

[48] Josel, L. (2025, May 12). *How Do I Create a Homework Space My Teen Will Want to Use?*. ADDitude Magazine. https://www.additudemag.com/homework-space-study-area-teen-adhd/

[49] Understood for All, Inc. (2023). *Classroom accommodations for ADHD*. Understood.org.

https://www.understood.org/en/articles/classroom-accommodations-for-adhd

[50] Hanson, C. (2025, May 25). *Managing Distractions With the Pomodoro Technique for ADHD.* Life Skills Advocate. https://lifeskillsadvocate.com/blog/pomodoro-technique-for-adhd/

[51] Yanoshik, J. (2024, August 8). *How to Create a Structured Schedule: Strategies for College Students with ADHD.* Weingarten Center. https://weingartencenter.universitylife.upenn.edu/creating-a-structured-schedule-with-adhd/

[52] Barnum C. (2025, March 12). *10 Time Management Strategies for ADHD Students.* A Mission For Michael. https://amfmtreatment.com/blog/10-time-management-strategies-for-adhd-students/

[53] Staff. (2025, April 16). *Struggling with ADHD? Here's How to Manage Your Time Effectively.* Amaze ABA. https://amazeaba.com/time-management-tips-for-adhd/

[54] Ellis, S. (2025, May 12). *The ADHD Homework Survival Guide for Parents.* APG Health. https://www.apghealth.com/the-adhd-homework-survival-guide-for-parents/

[55] Jacobson, R. (2023, November 06). *School Success Kit for Kids With ADHD.* Child Mind Institute. https://childmind.org/article/school-success-kit-for-kids-with-adhd/

[56] Impact Parents. (2019, April). *Strategies to Make Homework Easier for Kids and Parents.* Impact Parents.

https://impactparents.com/blog/adhd/strategies-to-make-homework-easier-for-kids-and-parents/

[57] Berger, R. (2022, October 25). *ADHD and Homework Management: Success Strategies*. Fun and Function. https://funandfunction.com/blog/ADHD-and-homework-management-success-strategies

[58] CHADD. (2018, May 01). *Homework Help for ADHD*. CHADD - Children and Adults with Attention-Deficit/Hyperactivity Disorder. https://chadd.org/for-parents/homework-help-for-adhd-2/

[59] BetterHelp Editorial Team. (2025, April 15). *IEPs vs 504 Plans: ADHD Accommodation Options For Students*. BetterHelp. https://www.betterhelp.com/advice/adhd/iep-vs-504-plan-adhd-accommodation-options-for-students/

[60] Cassata, C. (2022, August 24). *My Child has ADHD. Should We Have an IEP or 504 Plan?*. ADHD Online. https://adhdonline.com/articles/my-child-has-adhd-should-we-have-an-iep-or-504-plan/

[61] (n.d.) https://www.amherstpediatrics.com/storage/app/media/for-parents-iep-vs-504-whats-the-difference.pdf

[62] Smith Eibeler LLC. (2024, January 1). *Does a Student With ADHD Get a 504 Plan or an IEP?*. Jersey Employment Lawyers. https://www.jerseyemploymentlawyers.com/frequently-asked-questions/does-a-student-with-adhd-get-a-504-plan-or-an-iep/

[63] Coppa, F. (2025, March 17). *Effective Collaboration Between Parents and Teachers for ADHD Learners*. Frances Coppa. https://www.francescoppa.com/parents-and-teachers-collaboration/

[64] Jiang, Y., Montazeralsedgh, P., & Blair, C. (2020, April). *Home-School Collaboration: It's Important for Children with ADHD*. CHADD. https://chadd.org/adhd-news/adhd-news-educators/home-school-collaboration-its-important-for-children-with-adhd/

[65] Lifecare Wellness. (2023, December 15). *ADHD in School: A Parent's Guide to Collaboration with Educators*. Lifecare Wellness. https://www.lifecarewellness.us/post/adhd-in-school-a-parent-s-guide-to-collaboration-with-educators

[66] Sunbelt. (2023, June 16). *ADHD Accommodations and Strategies for Students*. Sunbelt Staffing. https://www.sunbeltstaffing.com/blog/adhd-accommodations-and-strategies-for-students/

[67] (n.d.) https://prntexas.org/wp-content/uploads/2024/07/TA-72-Accommodations-ADHD-Partners-Resource-Network.pdf

[68] (n.d.) https://education.wm.edu/centers/ttac/documents/packets/adhd.pdf

[69] (n.d.) https://vbc.edu/wp-content/uploads/2022/09/Classroom-Accommodations-Russell-Barkley.pdf

[70] Designer. (2024, July 28). *How to Support Siblings of Children with ADHD*. Harley Street Mental Health. https://hsmh.co.uk/blogs/how-to-support-siblings-of-children-with-adhd/

[71] Alpine Integrative Wellness. (2025, February 22). *Family Therapy for ADHD: Practical Strategies to Support Your Teen*. Alpine Integrative Wellness. https://alpineintegrativewellness.com/family-therapy-for-adhd/

[72] Saline S. (2025, May 11). *When ADHD Drains and Strains Sibling Relationships*. ADDitude Magazine. https://www.additudemag.com/sibling-relationships-adhd-families/

[73] Puster, M. (2025, July 23). *How to End Sibling Fighting Peacefully*. ADDitude Magazine. https://www.additudemag.com/siblings-fighting-conflict-resolution-adhd-family/

[74] Solandis Mental Health. (2023, December 15). *Navigating Family Life with ADHD: Strategies for Balance and Understanding*. Solandis Mental Health. https://www.solandismentalhealth.com/post/navigating-family-life-with-adhd-strategies-for-balance-and-understanding

[75] Pfiffner, L. J. (2014, October 1). *Behavior Management for School-Aged Children with ADHD*. PMC - US National Library of Medicine. https://pmc.ncbi.nlm.nih.gov/articles/PMC4167345/

[76] McQueen, J. (2024, June 18). *Family Therapy for Children With ADHD*. WebMD. https://www.webmd.com/add-adhd/childhood-adhd/childhood-adhd-family-therapy

[77] Paidipati C. P. (2017, January 11). *Parent and Family Processes Related to ADHD Management in Ethnically Diverse Youth*. Journal of the American Psychiatric Nurses Association. https://pmc.ncbi.nlm.nih.gov/articles/PMC5915362/

[78] Eldred, S. M. (2019, December 17). *When One of Your Kids Has ADHD and Your Others Don't.* HealthCentral. https://www.healthcentral.com/article/adhd-and-siblings

[79] CHADD. (2023, January 01). *Parenting a Child with ADHD.* CHADD - Children and Adults with Attention-Deficit/Hyperactivity Disorder. https://chadd.org/for-parents/overview/

[80] Hallowell E. M. (2025, June 18). *The ADHD Soul Shine Kit: Build Your Child's Self-Esteem.* ADDitude Magazine. https://www.additudemag.com/self-esteem-build-adhd-child-confidence/

[81] Hasan, S. M. (2022, May). *Parenting a Child With ADHD.* KidsHealth. https://kidshealth.org/en/parents/parenting-kid-adhd.html

[82] The Meadows Psychiatric Center. (2025, January 27). *Strategies for Supporting Children with ADHD.* The Meadows Psychiatric Center. https://themeadows.net/blog/strategies-for-supporting-children-with-adhd/

[83] San Pedro Pediatric Medical Group. (2024, August 23). *Effective Parenting Strategies for Children with ADHD: Managing Behavior and Encouraging Growth.* San Pedro Pediatric Medical Group. https://www.sanpedropediatricmedicalgroup.com/blog/effective-parenting-strategies-for-children-with-adhd-managing-behavior-and-encouraging-growth/

[84] Neumann, D. M. (2024, November). *9 Effective Strategies for Managing ADHD in Kids.* Wee Care Pediatrics.

https://weecarepediatrics.com/9-effective-strategies-for-managing-adhd-in-kids/

85 Centers for Disease Control and Prevention. (2024, October 22). *ADHD in the Classroom: Helping Children Succeed in School.* CDC. https://www.cdc.gov/adhd/treatment/classroom.html

86 Waters, L. (2017, December 11). *Pay Attention! How Strength-Based Parenting Can Help Your Child Stay Focused.* Lea Waters AM, PhD. https://www.leawaters.com/blog/pay-attention-how-strength-based-parenting-can-help-your-child-stay-focused

87 QbTech. (2023, October 15). *Optimize ADHD Treatment Approach Through a Strengths-Based Model of Care: Key Insights from our Webinar.* QbTech Blog. https://www.qbtech.com/blog/optimize-adhd-treatment-approach-through-a-strengths-based-model-of-care-key-insights-from-our-webinar/

88 OT4ADHD. (2024, January 02). *Using a Strength-Based Approach to Empower Learners with ADHD.* OT4ADHD. https://ot4adhd.com/2024/01/02/using-a-strength-based-approach-to-empower-learners-with-adhd/

89 Waters, L. (2019, September 24). *How to Be a Strength-Based Parent for Kids with Learning Differences.* Greater Good Magazine. https://greatergood.berkeley.edu/article/item/howtobeastrengthbasedparentforkidswithlearning_differences

90 Debinski, I. & Jiang, Y. (2024, April). *Understanding ADHD from a Strengths-Based Perspective.* CHADD. https://chadd.org/attention-article/understanding-adhd-from-a-strengths-based-perspective/

[91] Ruth A. (2025, February 20). *Conquer Time: Essential Tools for ADHD Time Management*. Calendar. https://www.calendar.com/blog/conquer-time-essential-tools-for-adhd-time-management/

[92] Bostic N. (2025, May 20). *5 to-do list apps that actually work with ADHD*. Zapier Blog. https://zapier.com/blog/adhd-to-do-list/

[93] ADDA Editorial Team. (2024, January 11). *6 Online ADHD Management Tools for Adults*. ADDA - Attention Deficit Disorder Association. https://add.org/adhd-tools-for-adults/

[94] The Holistic Time Coach. (2024, January 21). *10 Best ADHD Tools For Time Management, Productivity, & Organization*. The Holistic Time Coach. https://www.theholistictimecoach.com/time-management-blog/adhd-time-management-tools

[95] Understood. (2023). *7 Apps to Help Teens With ADHD Manage Everyday Challenges*. Understood.org. https://www.understood.org/en/articles/apps-to-help-teens-with-adhd-manage-challenges

[96] DiProperzio, L. (2021, March 23). *The Best Apps and Online Resources for Kids with ADHD*. Rockland Parent. https://www.rocklandparent.com/article/apps-and-resources-for-kids-with-adhd

[97] The ADHD Centre. (2023, November 29). *Empowering young minds – 10 apps for children under 10*. The ADHD Centre. https://www.adhdcentre.co.uk/empowering-young-minds-10-apps-for-children-under-10/

98 Josel, L. (2025, July 7). *Study Apps for Kids with Learning Differences & ADHD*. Smart Kids with Learning Disabilities. https://www.smartkidswithld.org/blog/study-apps-for-kids-with-learning-differences-adhd/

99 Lindberg, S. (2022, February 11). *10 Tips for Helping Kids with ADHD Manage Screen Time*. Healthline. https://www.healthline.com/health/adhd/10-tips-for-helping-kids-with-adhd-manage-screen-time

100 Pierce, R. (2023, March 27). *ADHD and Screen Time Management: 11 Techniques for Success*. Life Skills Advocate. https://lifeskillsadvocate.com/blog/11-tips-for-creating-boundaries-around-screen-time-with-adhd/

101 McQueen, J. (2024, June 14). *Screen Time and ADHD in Children*. WebMD. https://www.webmd.com/add-adhd/childhood-adhd/childhood-adhd-screen-time

102 Understood for All, Inc. (2023). *How to help kids with ADHD manage screen time*. Understood.org. https://www.understood.org/en/articles/at-a-glance-helping-kids-with-adhd-manage-screen-time

103 Raising Children Network. (2025, July 28). *Self-advocacy for your child with disability, autism or ADHD*. Raising Children Network. https://raisingchildren.net.au/autism/school-play-work/school/self-advocacy-children-teenagers-disability-autism

104 Schultz J. (2025, June 19). *A 6-Step Plan for Teaching ADHD Self-Advocacy Skills*. ADDitude Magazine.

https://www.additudemag.com/self-awareness-activities-self-advocacy-skills-adhd/

105 EducateAble. (2024, November 18). *Strong Self-Advocacy: A Key to Thriving with ADHD*. EducateAble. https://educateable.in/2024/11/18/strong-self-advocacy-a-key-to-thriving-with-adhd/

106 Huntington Learning Center. (2023, September 28). *The Importance of Teaching Self-Advocacy Skills to Children with ADHD*. Huntington Helps. https://huntingtonhelps.com/blog/the-importance-of-teaching-self-advocacy-skills-to-children-with-adhd/

107 Shenoy, R. (2025, April 28). *Self-Advocacy Scripts to Empower Neurodivergent Kids: A Research-Backed Guide for Parents*. Monster Math. https://www.monstermath.app/blog/self-advocacy-scripts-to-empower-neurodivergent-kids-a-research-backed-guide-for-parents-cma0yyy8m003nw91uu0az102t

108 Shenoy, R. (2025, May 23). *Money Matters: 5 Hands-On Money-Learning Activities for ADHD Kids*. Monster Math. https://www.monstermath.app/blog/money-matters-5-hands-on-money-learning-activities-for-adhd-kids-cmb0m1xh8002smjqlsuz89gmg

109 Sippl, A. (2024, June 12). *Understanding the ADHD Tax: The Unseen Cost of Executive Dysfunction*. Life Skills Advocate. https://lifeskillsadvocate.com/blog/understanding-the-adhd-tax-the-unseen-cost-of-executive-dysfunction/

[110] ADDA Editorial Team. (2023, November 17). *Managing Money With ADHD-Friendly Strategies*. ADDA - Attention Deficit Disorder Association. https://add.org/adhd-friendly-financial-management-yes-and-its-not-what-you-think/

[111] Shenoy, R. (2025, March 26). *Your ADHD Kid Isn't Bad With Money — Here's the Real Issue*. Monster Math. https://www.monstermath.app/blog/your-adhd-kid-isnt-bad-with-money-heres-the-real-issue-cm8pvu9yk001plvllay6idsnn

[112] Community Psychiatric Centers. (2025, March 17). *Helping Teens with Autism and ADHD Transition into Adulthood*. Help For Your Child. https://helpforyourchild.com/helping-teens-with-autism-and-adhd-transition-into-adulthood/

[113] Brown L. W. (2023). *Transitioning to Independence for Adolescents with ADHD*. CHADD. https://chadd.org/continuing-education/transitioning-to-independence-for-adolescents-with-adhd/

[114] Ford T. (2020, January 9). *Transitional care for young adults with ADHD: transforming potential upheaval into smooth progression*. Epidemiology and Psychiatric Sciences. https://pmc.ncbi.nlm.nih.gov/articles/PMC7214737/

[115] Sibley, M. H. (2023, April). *Launching Successful Young Adults with ADHD*. CHADD. https://chadd.org/adhd-news/adhd-news-caregivers/attention-launching-successful-young-adults-with-adhd/

[116] Taylor-Klaus, E. & Dempster, D. (2022, April 13). *Four Steps to Independence: How to Support (Not Enable) a Child with ADHD*. ADDitude Magazine.

https://www.additudemag.com/slideshows/enabling-vs-supporting-helping-adhd-kids-be-independent/

Thank You for Reading!

I hope you found *Working with the ADHD Brain (Parent Edition): A Parent's Guide to Building Focus, Organization, and Academic Success* helpful and enjoyable!

Your feedback is invaluable to me and helps others discover this book.

If you could take a moment to **leave a review**, I'd greatly appreciate it. Scan the QR code below to leave your review:

Thank you,

Patty R. Adams

www.ingramcontent.com/pod-product-compliance
Lightning Source LLC
Chambersburg PA
CBHW061756120626
46550CB00005B/2018